THE WORLD'S TOUGHEST RACES

FROM THE MOST EXTREME TO THE DOWNRIGHT WEIRD

ALI CLARKE

summersdale

THE WORLD'S
TOUGHEST
RACES

THE WORLD'S TOUGHEST RACES

Copyright © Summersdale Publishers Ltd, 2015

Research by Jennifer Barclay, Steven Gauge and Ian Robert Smith.

Summersdale Publishers Ltd
46 West Street
Chichester
West Sussex
PO19 1RP
UK

www.summersdale.com

Printed and bound in the Czech Republic

ISBN: 978-1-84953-730-8

Substantial discounts on bulk quantities of Summersdale books are available to corporations, professional associations and other organisations. For details contact Nicky Douglas by telephone: +44 (0) 1243 756902, fax: +44 (0) 1243 786300 or email: nicky@summersdale.com.

CONTENTS

CHAPTER 4 – STONE

CHAPTER 5 – MULTI-DISCIPLINE

CHAPTER 6 – EXTREME WHEELS

? CHAPTER 7 – WEIRDEST

INTRODUCTION

Adventure races and endurance challenges have grown at a phenomenal rate in the past decade, with thousands of men and women travelling to all corners of the earth to take part in events that will test their limits. If you're reading this book, you've probably considered doing the same.

We have scoured the top ten lists, hunted down the unusual challenges and read some moving and hilarious accounts in order to compile this selection of the world's toughest, weirdest and most extreme races – and to find out what is so special about each one that keeps people coming back for more. We've looked at the coldest and the hottest, races by sea and over the highest mountains in the world, through jungle and deserts. There are epic foot races, canoe and kayak races, swim challenges and mountain biking events; and then there are some more unusual ones, and some multi-discipline events including climbing and orienteering.

So, what is it about the 'sufferfest' that appeals?

Part of it is the location. Some of these events offer an opportunity to visit remote corners of the world that very few have the chance to experience in their lifetime. The spectacular physical beauty of the place alone can be breathtaking and the interaction with local people produces memorable moments. Often as we read about a race, we catch ourselves dreaming and wondering if we could do it ourselves.

Part of it is sharing suffering and exhilaration with those around you; the camaraderie is remarkable.

But more than that, these extreme challenges offer us something that is lacking from our everyday lives: where we drift from office to supermarket, where we get in our cars to drive to the gym and use our smartphones to tell us how to get around. We want to be surprised, to have our self-sufficiency tested and to use our own power and wits. We want our bodies to be pushed to the very limits, to know if we have the mental resilience to keep going. We want that total immersion in an unforgiving natural environment – something far removed from our highly mechanised society. Many competitors find that the sense of achievement fills a gap and spurs them on to a greater appreciation of life.

Although many of these events are races, they are about much more than just speed. Getting to the finish line is important, but it's the experience that counts. How much do you think you could endure and survive? Read on, and decide.

CHAPTER 1
ICE

NORTH POLE MARATHON

What is it? The World's Coolest Marathon®

Location: On the melting layer of ice that floats around the Arctic Ocean

Established: 2002

Held: Annually in April

Equipment: Base layers, insulating layers, wind-shell layer, gloves, balaclava, mask, thermal hat, neck gaiter, ski goggles

Distance: 26.2 miles (42 km)

Obstacles: Wind-chill temperatures of more than –30°C, loose snow and ice. Don't worry about polar bears; it's far too cold for them

For the opportunity to run a marathon on the top of the world, you need to head for Svalbard peninsula off the coast of Norway. From there you will be flown to the North Pole, just so long as the race organisers have been able to find an ice block big enough to build the runway for the Antonov aircraft to land on. The exact course depends on how the ice has shaped up over the previous year, but typically you will do 10 laps of a 2.6 mile (4.2 km) circuit, finishing up at the ceremonial North Pole, where all the lines of longitude meet. There is a large heated tent where you can warm up again after each lap if necessary.

The exact race location is rather unpredictable, as is the terrain. A mix of solid ice and loose snow will drain your reserves and make it very difficult to establish a rhythm in your run. However, veteran explorer Sir Ranulph Fiennes, who completed the North Pole Marathon in 2004, declared that with the right preparation, anyone who has run a marathon should be able to cope: 'Just make sure you bring some dark glasses.'

The entire course floats around the magnetic North Pole over the course of the race but the organisers promise that you won't notice or start to feel seasick. When everyone has finished the race, it's all into a helicopter for a quick photo opportunity at wherever the magnetic pole happens to be at that precise moment.

PROFILE

Australian runner Demelza Farr and her boyfriend James Alderson put their names down for the 2012 race. There were 11 women runners in a field of 46 athletes from 15 countries. Demelza had not had the best preparation for the race and a bad training run left her with a painful back during the race. Although she thought that she might not finish, with her boyfriend by her side throughout the race she ended up as the fastest woman, completing the course in 5 hours, 9 minutes and 43 seconds.

James, her boyfriend, may have had his mind on other things during the race. He had secretly been carrying an engagement ring with him around the 26.2 mile (42 km) course. As the couple crossed the finishing line together he got down on one knee to propose. The video recording of Demelza's reaction became an internet sensation – she said yes, of course – and the happy couple went on to run a marathon at the South Pole for their honeymoon.

STATISTICS

 Total number of finishers so far:
Approximately 350

 Nations represented: 40

 Fastest man: Thomas Maguire (Ireland), 3 hours 36 minutes 10 seconds (2007)

 Fastest woman: Anne-Marie Flammersfeld (Germany), 4 hours 52 minutes 45 seconds (2014)

 Coldest race: 2002 – in the inaugural run the wind-chill temperature was recorded at –60°C

❄ ARROWHEAD 135 ULTRAMARATHON

What is it? A solo race through winter forest

Location: North Woods, Minnesota, USA

Established: 2005

Held: Annually in early February

Equipment: Either a snow bike with panniers, skis with rucksack or, for walkers, a sled containing food, water and cold-weather gear to enable competitors to survive for 60-odd hours

Distance: 135 miles (217 km)

Obstacles: Extreme cold (2014's starting temp at 7 a.m. in the town of International Falls was measured at –37°C), an undulating course, solitude, lack of sleep

Now over a decade old, the Arrowhead 135 Ultramarathon proclaims itself 'historically [the] coldest gosh darn race anyplace even the Arctic'. It is certainly a race of extremes, in which competitors either ride, ski or run through undulating and wooded country in the far north of the American state of Minnesota, the 'Icebox of the Nation'. In 2015 local rider Jorden Wakeley won the bike leg in a thrilling finish that saw the first four riders cross the line with only a second separating each of them.

Devised by locals, the race was born out of the challenging conditions, dedicated to the promotion of human-powered ultra-endurance events in northern Minnesota's physically stunning Arrowhead region. In order to compete, racers must meet stringent qualifications which entail experience of a similar type of race (full details are given on the application form). For their own safety during the race, they are obliged to carry a large load of equipment including a –20°F sleeping bag, an insulated sleeping pad, a bivvy bag or tent, 8 oz (225 g) of fuel and at least 3,000 calories of food at all times.

The Arrowhead 135 begins near the US–Canadian border and finishes near Lake Vermilion where the trail bisects Highway 77. Relatively flat in its northern portion, its southern part consists of rolling hills punctuated by lakes and streams, and heavily timbered with a mix of hardwood and conifers. The trail is well-marked and in good condition, and features a series of mandatory checkpoints where competitors can get hot food and drink, dry their clothes, defrost water (and often food) that has frozen and even catch an hour or two of sleep in a bunk. Along with the occasional official on a snowmobile, the checkpoints also provide racers with information on weather conditions and the progress of fellow competitors.

For many racers, the goal is not so much to win as to complete the race. The elements provide the main opposition. Intense cold is always an issue, while other obstacles include snow, ice, wind and the rolling landscape. Competitors must also be able to deal with solitude, as for much of the race they will be alone. The occasional appearance of wolves and their tracks provides another mental challenge. A special feature of the Arrowhead 135 is the Ernest Shackleton award. This commemorates the British explorer's 1914 Trans-Antarctic expedition and, celebrating the qualities of endurance, fortitude and persistence, is given to the athlete who endures longest in finishing the course.

PROFILE

Hailing from Texas, Jim Kronjaeger always knew it was going to be an uphill battle running an ultramarathon in America's snowy north. Inspired by stories of polar exploration and mountain adventures consumed in his youth, and considering the Arrowhead 135 the next best thing to climbing Mount Everest or journeying to the South Pole, Kronjaeger qualified for the 2012 event by running a 100-mile (161-km) foot race at Rocky Raccoon in 2011. After failing to finish both that race and the 2013 Arrowhead due to snow, 'pruned feet' and other complications, he went into the 2014 race following months of intense training and a total rethink in terms of equipment, paring his load down to a minimum and paying particular attention to the care of his feet.

Kronjaeger was not a high-profile athlete or potential race winner. Rather he was one of those journeyman athletes whose goal in the race was simply to finish. Tellingly, on the side of his sled Kronjaeger had inscribed the mantra: 'Eddie would go'. This was inspired by the legendary Hawaiian surfer Eddie Aikau who, Kronjaeger writes, 'would venture into the sea to rescue people when the waves were so high that no-one else would dare'.

Along with the fearsome cold that knocked so many competitors out of the 2014 event, Kronjaeger struggled with exhaustion, blisters and chafing, legs that at times ceased to respond, dehydration and, crucially, hallucinations arising from sleep deprivation. Battling night winds that lowered the temperature to –40°C, Kronjaeger summarised the elements of the Arrowhead 135 as 'strength, endurance, solitude, survival' and, in assessing his tactics, revised the acronym DNF – 'did not finish' – to 'do nothing fatal'.

In the last stages of the race, Kronjaeger suffered the misfortune of missing the markers at a crossroads and taking a wrong turn, which meant backtracking a crucial few miles, delaying his finish. His time of 58 hours 30 minutes just enabled him to qualify as a finisher.

STATISTICS

 Weather: Conditions in 2014 were abysmal, resulting in less than a third of the field finishing

 Men's run 2015: Marcus Berggren (Sweden) slashed nearly three hours off the previous course record, crossing the line in 34 hours 20 minutes

 Women's run 2015: Sue Lucas (Canada) finished in 42 hours 31 minutes, 5.5 hours under the previous women's record. Lucas placed eighth overall

Youngest ever competitor to win: Jorden Wakeley (USA), 2015, aged 24, 15 hours (bike)

# 6633 ULTRA

What is it? An extreme ultramarathon, with each competitor carrying or pulling their kit by sled – the 'toughest, coldest and windiest extreme ultramarathon on the planet'

Location: Canadian Arctic between Eagle Plains, Yukon and Tuktoyaktuk, Northwest Territories on the banks of the Arctic Ocean

Established: 2007

Held: Annually in March

Equipment: Sled, camping and cooking equipment, thermal gear, goggles, face mask, etc.

Distance: 120/350 miles (193/563 km)

Obstacles: Sub-zero temperatures

Those who finish the full 350 miles (563 km) of the 6633 Ultra join a very exclusive club. Fewer than 30 athletes compete annually in this non-stop self-sufficient foot race crossing the line of the Arctic Circle, with about half opting to continue for the longer race to the banks of the Arctic Ocean at Tuktoyaktuk. Competitors carry all food, cooking utensils, clothing and other kit and must contend with high winds and blinding snow. 6633 are the latitude coordinates of the Arctic Circle.

The race starts at the Eagle Plains Hotel, 225 miles (362 km) from the Dawson Junction on the Klondike Highway, setting out through stunted Arctic forest and then into some of the most inhospitable landscape on the planet, including Hurricane Alley, with Katabatic winds that regularly blow over trucks and can reduce humans to a slow crawl. Winds continue to dog the steep ascent to Wright Pass and the 'ice road', a frozen river. The biggest challenge is said to be the mental one at Inuvik, where competitors face barren, pure-white landscapes at the finish.

Two drop-bags of essential gear are allowed for those competing in the longer race at Fort McPherson and Inuvik, approximately one-third and two-thirds of the way, and all competitors are allowed a bag at the finish for spare warm clothing. Checkpoints guarantee to provide only hot water and shelter.

PROFILE

When experienced ultra runner Mimi Anderson undertook the 6633 Ultra in 2007, it was her first venture into the cold. During the race that year, temperatures averaged −40°C, with the wind chill one day taking it as low as −59°C. The Northern Lights put on a smoky green spectacle every night, however, bouncing around in the sky and lighting the way.

As she approached Caribou Creek in the second half of the race, she started to hallucinate: 'I saw an elephant, hundreds of men on skidoos about to attack me, men carrying guns...' She was told by the medic at the checkpoint that she must rest for six hours because of fatigue, or could face being withdrawn.

It was difficult to keep her hands warm when overmitts had to be removed to take out food, so one of the highlights was being given a sandwich by three men in a van who stopped to talk to her on the ice road, providing her with a new lease of energy. The lowest point of the race was reaching the outskirts of Tuktoyaktuk and being told she still had 7 miles (11 km) to complete, when her body was freezing. But her son ran that section with her for morale, and when she reached the finish there were locals in cars and skidoos shouting encouragement, and she had won the race – 24 hours ahead of the next competitor.

Her father died while she was competing in the race: 'I know he was there with me,' she said. It was an extraordinary achievement for a woman who suffered for years with anorexia. Now a grandmother, running has given Mimi the ability to believe in herself again.

STATISTICS

 Distance between checkpoints for rest and food:
23–70 miles (37–113 km)

 Record holder for 120-mile (193-km) race:
Kevin Hollings, 2013, 34 hours 35 minutes

 Record holder for 350-mile (563-km) race:
Mimi Anderson, 2007, 143 hours 25 minutes

THE WORLD'S TOUGHEST RACES

 Number of entrants competing to reach Arctic Ocean in 2013: 24

 Number of finishers at Arctic Ocean in 2013: 4

Total number of finishers who had reached the Arctic Ocean prior to 2013: 6

Temperature range at start: Anything from –45°C to a balmy –32°C

NORSEMAN XTREME TRIATHLON

What is it? The 'ultimate triathlon on planet earth'

Location: Norway

Established: 2003

Held: Annually in August

Equipment: Wetsuit, neoprene socks and cap recommended, bike with lights and helmet, two backpacks containing warm clothing, flashlight/headlamp, food and drink, mobile phone, cash for cafeteria, support team

Distance: 140 miles (226 km)

Obstacles: Fjord to peak – sea level to 6,070 ft (1,850 m); total ascent 9,843 ft (5,000 m)

The Norseman route begins with a legendary 4-m jump from the ferry into the dark, deep, cold Hardangerfjord in west Norway, which is surrounded by snowy mountains. The landscape only gets more spectacular from there. The temperature on race morning is usually 13–15°C, depending on snowmelt and rivers and nearby hydropower production, which affects water temperature. Wetsuits are mandatory for the 2.4-mile (3.8-km) swim. This is followed by a bike ride of 112 miles (180 km) crossing the mountain plateau of Hardangervidda along national roads and country roads to Austbygd at Lake Tinnsjøen.

Competitors then run 26.2 miles (42 km), of which the first 15.5 miles (25 km) is fairly flat, ending in a steep climb of 10.7 miles (17.2 km) to the 6,070-ft (1,850-m) high top of Mount Gaustatoppen, the final section being on rocky trail. Cut-off times prevent participants continuing alone on the mountains after dark as conditions can be dangerous.

The idea of the Norseman started in 2001 when Paal Hårek Stranheim and Bent Olav Olsen were lamenting the fact that only nine Norwegians had competed in triathlon events the previous year. Stranheim wanted to create a 'completely different race' through some of Norway's most beautiful nature, with the experience 'more important than the finish time', and family and friends offering support. The weather can be beautiful and you might see porpoises, orcas or reindeer. But he also wanted it to be the hardest Ironman race on earth.

Norseman Xtreme Triathlon is organised by the 20 or so members of the Hardangervidda Triathlon Klubb, who are also the main crew of the race. In 2014 for the first time since 2004 Norwegians topped both the men's and women's class: Allan Hovda (10 hours 52 minutes 7 seconds) and Line Foss (12 hours 56 minutes 27 seconds). The water temperature in the fjord was warmer than average, 16°C, but competitors had to reckon with headwinds, rain, hail and thick fog.

PROFILE

While the swim is statistically the most dangerous part of any triathlon, it's the steep final ascent of the mountain at the end of the Norseman that is strictly controlled for safety reasons. While the entire race is restricted to

250 athletes a year, only the first 160 competitors are allowed past the 20-mile (32-km) mark to finish on top of the mountain. Those arriving later complete the distance at plateau level. Those finishing on top claim their prize of a black T-shirt, while those finishing at plateau level receive a white T-shirt. So far 35 women and 466 men have earned the black finisher shirt.

In 2005 and 2007 the race could not continue to the top of the Mount Gaustatoppen because of snow, cold rain and heavy winds. In normal conditions, the air temperature on the high parts of the mountain is likely to be from 2–12°C. A mountain safety checkpoint at 23 miles (37.5 km) ensures participants are properly equipped to continue according to the rules of the manual. A support crew is mandatory to continue up 'Zombie Hill' – so called because its sheer steepness slows racers down into exhausted, speechless automatons – to the final ascent: no athlete is allowed past Stavsro, the mountain safety checkpoint, alone.

Peter Oom came tenth in the Norseman 2014. Having also competed in the Celtman and Swissman, he said the local athletes had an advantage by knowing the routes, and riding the course before would have helped.

At 20 miles (32 km) there was a checkpoint, and the racer ahead of Peter had stopped. Peter and his support guy, Thor, understood that everyone was being told to stop for five minutes. Then he realised: 'The guy in front had actually a five-minute penalty to serve.' He had lost a few minutes for no reason, and was already angry when he reached the next checkpoint, and found Thor wasn't ready. On the final stretch, the terrain was getting worse and the fog thicker and thicker. He heard voices but had no idea where they were coming from. Suddenly the finish line loomed out of the fog. He'd achieved tenth place, not in the top five as he'd hoped. But lessons had been learned, he was happy with his performance, and was: 'Most of all happy with my wife, and that she lives with me doing these crazy things.'

STATISTICS

 Number of athletes who competed in the first Norseman Xtreme Triathlon in 2003: 21

 Number of finishers in 2003: 19

 Fastest time in 2003: 12 hours 48 minutes (Christian Houge-Thiis)

 Male/female ratio: 85/15

 Percentage of Norwegian athletes: 50 per cent

 Fastest ever finish: 10 hours 30 minutes 9 seconds

 Slowest ever finish: 22 hours 5 minutes 20 seconds

Statistics for 2014:

 Fastest man: Allan Hovda completed 18 minutes ahead of Lars Christian Vold

 Fastest woman: Line Foss completed 43 minutes ahead of the second-place woman Maggie Rush

 Number of applicants: 1,953 from 51 countries

 Number of athletes who competed: 260 from 30 countries

 Total number of finishers: 247

ANTARCTIC ICE MARATHON

What is it? Marathon run on snow and ice

Location: The foothills of Antarctica's Ellsworth Mountains

Established: 2005

Held: Annually in November

Equipment: Cold-weather gear including wind pants, down jacket and insulated boots

Distance: 26.2 miles (42 km)

Obstacles: Snow and ice, intense cold which with wind chill can fall as low as –25°C

Testimonials by runners who have completed the Antarctic Ice Marathon invariably speak of the otherworldly beauty of the polar landscape against which the race is conducted. Mountains, glaciers, pure, cold, clean-smelling air and the pristine whiteness of snow and ice are invariably cited as the highlights of what many former runners describe as an awesome, once-in-a-lifetime opportunity. Held at 80 degrees south, just a few hundred kilometres from the South Pole at the foot of the Ellsworth Mountains, the Antarctic Ice Marathon can lay claim to be both the southernmost marathon in the world and the only marathon to be held on the Antarctic mainland.

Organised by Polar Running Adventures (which is also responsible for the Antarctic 100k race and the world's most northerly marathon, the North Pole Marathon), the Antarctic

Ice Marathon is, as you would imagine, logistically complex. It is also one of the world's more elite marathons, in which athletes pay an enormous sum of money (the entry fee for 2016 is over €11,000) to have themselves flown by private jet from Chile to Union Glacier, Antarctica, where, after landing on a naturally occurring ice runway, they are housed in double-insulated tents and wined and dined for the three nights they are there. The race takes place on a 26.2-mile (42-km) marked course that has been prepared in advance with the support of snowmobiles, aid stations and medical personnel.

Upon completion of the marathon, the entrant's race fee also gets them a flight back to Punta Arenas in Chile, a medal, T-shirts, patches, certificate, professional photographs and a short film of the event for private use. Aside from competing on what may reasonably be termed 'the last frontier of marathons', the other attraction of the Ice Marathon is that it makes runners eligible for membership in the coveted Seven Continents Club.

In this land beyond the range of penguins, who decline to venture so far south, competitors must be prepared to deal with all manner of challenges, from snow and ice underfoot, to extreme temperatures and biting winds, to the eerie and possibly disconcerting emptiness of a hushed white world devoid of spectators.

PROFILE

When in 2010 American runner Sarah Oliphant embarked upon the Antarctic Ice Marathon, she had already run marathons on six of the seven continents as well as the North Pole Marathon. Her completion of the race, in third place in the women's division with the time of 6 hours 32 minutes 48 seconds, gained her entry into both the Seven Continents Club and the Marathon Grand Slam Club. At 15 years of age she was the youngest person ever to achieve the feat.

Coming in behind Sarah, with a time of 6 hours 37 minutes 45 seconds, was her father, Arnold. At 51, Arnold was a scientist with a doctorate in genetics. Four years previously he had spent two years confined to his bed by rheumatoid arthritis, from which he gradually improved his condition through diet and exercise. He began his rehabilitation on a home elliptical trainer, working in sessions of five and six minutes at a time. Eventually he reached the stage where he was able to leave the house and walk around the block.

Running in the company of his daughter followed. In what is surely a perfect example of the old adage that great achievements begin with small steps, they started with small and manageable jogs around the block, gradually increasing their distance as the months went on.

Then, in January 2008, father and daughter began marathon training. This led to them competing in the Utah Marathon six months later. For Arnold it was a mighty achievement. Sarah, meanwhile, 12 years old at the time, had experienced difficulty finding a marathon that would allow someone her age to compete.

According to Arnold, age isn't a consideration when running a marathon. In his opinion, adults are far too inclined to use age as a barrier to stop young people from achieving their dreams. Certainly marathons held no terrors for the 15-year-old Sarah. 'I like it when it's hard because it makes me happy,' she said. 'I feel joy running in that type of environment.'

Conditions for the 2010 Ice Marathon were ideal, with clear skies and the temperature hovering around 14°C. The sun hung around the whole time, bathing competitors in 24-hour light. A couple of days after the race, just for the hell of it, Sarah and some friends travelled to southern Chile and ran in the Punta Arenas marathon. Clearly, at her age, problems like stiffness and muscle soreness are unknown.

STATISTICS

 Men's record: 3 hours 34 minutes 47 seconds, set by Petr Vabroušek (2013)

 Women's record: 4 hours 20 minutes 2 seconds, set by Fiona Oakes (2013)

 The race initially took place at Patriot Hills in Antarctica but in 2010 the venue changed to Union Glacier

 In 2007, a wheelchair competitor, William Tan, completed a marathon distance on the airport runway

 The sister race of the Antarctica Ice Marathon is the North Pole Marathon, which is the most northerly marathon on earth

IDITAROD TRAIL INVITATIONAL

What is it? A race by bike, ski or foot, along a dog-sled route

Location: Alaska

Established: 2000

Held: Annually in March

Equipment: Fat-tyred bike, cross-country skis or snow shoes (depending on your choice of mode of transport), sleeping bag, camping stove and gas canisters, food and a small sled to drag everything along with you

Distance: 350 miles (563 km) or 1,000 miles (1,609 km)

Obstacles: Thick snow, ice, blowholes (terrifying localised blizzards) and charging moose

One of the world's greatest races is the Iditarod, across Alaska from Anchorage to Nome, but most people complete that race with the aid of a team of sled dogs to pull them along. A brave few choose to complete the course entirely under their own steam. The course is so tough that the organisers limit the race to just 50 people each year and every one of them has to have completed a qualifying ultramarathon before being considered.

The Iditarod dog-sled race began in the early 1970s in an attempt to preserve the fading tradition of dog mushing. Over the decades that followed a few attempts were made to run or ride sections of dogsled route without dogs. However, it wasn't until 2000 that anyone attempted the 1,000-mile distance. The race was known as the Iditarod Impossible, but Mike Curiak managed to complete it in just over 15 days with six other cyclists finishing behind him over the next six days. Canadian Dave Norona set off on skis and finished an unofficial 33 days, 4 hours and 30 minutes later.

There is no set course. The route just becomes the path through the ice that the competitors chose to take. There are checkpoints along the route and competitors will post bags full of provisions to various village post offices and other points on the way. The route changes on alternate years to minimise the impact on the local villages. On even years they take a northern route and on odd years they take a southern route. The dog teams start off a couple of days behind the cyclists and normally overtake the runners and riders along the way – though in 2014, benefiting from warm days and less snow than usual, cyclist Jeff Oakley made it to all the way to Nome just before the first huskies started to arrive.

PROFILE

While there are just over 40 people who have successfully completed the 1,000-mile (1,609-km) course, Tim Hewitt is in a league of his own, having run the full length of the course no less than eight times. An employment lawyer from Pennsylvania, Tim is one of the toughest ultra-endurance athletes in the world. A gymnast at college, Tim took up running socially when he was at law school but didn't start to compete properly until he was in his 40s. He started winning ultramarathons in the 50–60 age group and set a course record for a 100-mile (161-km) race on the Iditarod trail in 2000.

Tim became tantalised by the prospect of the Iditarod Impossible and entered the second 1,000-mile race in 2001. He was vying for the lead with fellow Pennsylvanian Tom Jarding for most of the race but two-thirds of the way through something went badly wrong. As he was focusing on a twinkling light in the distance, he stepped into a hole and a sharp pain shot through his toes and his knee. He had a stress fracture in his tibia, three-quarters of the way through the bone. Unbelievably he kept going, crawling on his hands and knees for uphill sections of the route. Eventually he finished along with Tom Jarding, the only other race finisher on foot, after a total of 26 days 20 hours 46 minutes.

In other years Tim has been caught in blowholes that have left him unable to move because of the strong winds. He has witnessed the moisture in his breath forming into snow as he spoke to a fellow competitor. On one journey he saw a fireball streaking through the sky. His wife Loreen also competes and in 2014 the two of them completed the course together. What is the secret of his success? Tim says, 'Being successful in this race requires a certain degree of stubbornness and unwillingness to give in.' That and a degree of flexibility to cope with whatever the course might throw at you.

STATISTICS

Northern route

 Bike record: 10 days 2 hours 53 minutes (Jeff Oatley, 2014)

 Foot record: 20 days 14 hours 45 minutes (Tom Jarding, 2010)

 Women's bike record: 17 days 6 hours 25 minutes (Ausilia Vistarini, 2014)

 Women's foot record: 26 days 6 hours 59 minutes (Loreen Hewitt, 2014)

Southern route

 Bike record: 17 days, 6 hours (Jay Petervary, 2011)

 Foot record: 20 days, 7 hours, 17 minutes (Tim Hewitt, 2011)

 Women's bike record: 18 days, 6 hours, 30 minutes (Tracey Petervary, 2011)

 Women's foot record: 30 days, 12 hours, 10 minutes (Shawn McTaggart, 2013)

 Calories burned per racer per day: 30,000

 Pounds gained by Tim Hewitt in preparation for the race in 2011: 8

 Pounds lost by Tim Hewitt during the race in 2011: 15

CHAPTER 2
WATER

MOLOKAI 2 OAHU PADDLEBOARD WORLD CHAMPIONSHIPS

What is it? A c. five-hour paddleboard race in the Pacific Ocean

Location: Hawaii

Established: 1997

Held: Annually in July

Equipment: Paddleboard, paddle (if entering the stand-up category), support vehicle

Distance: 32 miles (51 km)

Obstacles: Jellyfish, flying fish, sharks and waves up to 12 ft high

---

When Captain Cook turned up in Hawaii in 1778, his ship's artist, John Webber, sketched one of the islanders lying on a board paddling through the surf. A couple of centuries later, paddleboarding has become another great sport providing gruelling challenges for endurance enthusiasts from all over the world.

The big race of the year is between the Hawaiian islands of Molokai and Oahu. The 32-mile (51-km) course takes paddlers across one of the most treacherous stretches of water in the Pacific. Known to locals as the Ka'iwi Channel, which translates as the 'Channel of Bones', huge ocean swells are squeezed between the two landmasses.

After a group prayer, the competitors all set off together, some lying down on the boards and paddling with their hands, others standing up and paddling with an oar. After an hour most of the competitors find themselves alone in the ocean with just their support crew behind them but with no other paddlers in sight.

According to Scott Gamble, who finished third in 2014, 'The race isn't won at the start of the race. Realistically the race doesn't start until you are three hours in and that's when your body really starts to hurt.' Around the four- and five-hour mark the racers start coming together again as they approach the finish line. The winner picks up a $3,000 cheque but all the participants are cheered across the line and then everyone heads to the Outrigger Canoe Club for the after-party. Aloha!

PROFILE

Mark Matheson's life changed somewhat when he found himself face down in the grass having just fallen off a hotel balcony four storeys above. Paralysed from the chest down, a few years later he was encouraged by Hawaiian non-profit group AccesSurf to try paddleboarding.

'It was really just for grins,' said Matheson, 'and then it turned into something much bigger.'

His first attempt in 2010 to complete the Molokai 2 Oahu challenge ended when his support boat broke down after six hours. The rules insist that all competitors have a support vessel with them for the entire crossing.

The next year Mark was back with sponsorship from a sunglasses company, a new custom-built board and not one support boat, but two. He completed the race in 9 hours 55 minutes 53 seconds to the biggest cheers of the day. 'The definition of success,' Matheson said, 'has always been making it to the starting line.'

STATISTICS

 Men's prone fastest time: 4 hours 40 minutes 31 seconds (Jamie Mitchell, Australia, 2011)

 Men's stand-up fastest time: 4 hours 8 minutes 8 seconds (Connor Baxter, Hawaii, 2014)

 Women's prone fastest time: 5 hours 22 minutes 31 seconds (Jordan Mercer, Australia, 2011)

 Women's stand-up fastest time: 4 hours 55 minutes 2 seconds (Talia Gangini, Hawaii, 2012)

 Most consecutive wins (men): 10 – Jamie Mitchell from 2002–11

 Most consecutive wins (women): 8 – Kanesa Duncan from 2001–10

11-CITY SUP TOUR

What is it? Stand-up paddleboard (SUP) race

Location: Friesland, Netherlands

Established: 2009

Held: Annually in September

Equipment: Stand-up paddleboard, single-hull, 14 ft or under, and single-blade paddle

Distance: 136 miles (220 km)

Obstacles: Changeable weather with hot, clear conditions giving way to rain, wind and thunderstorms

Holland's 11-City SUP Tour is by far the longest event of its type in the world. It was a tough call even in its original format in which competitors covered the distance in five individual stages spread over five days. In 2014, however, race organisers decided to make things even tougher by introducing what they called a 'non-stop' category: the chance to cover the entire course in one bite, without indulging in pleasantries like rest or sleep.

It is the latest development in a race that is continuously evolving. In 2009 the race was an invitational event in which athletes with the right credentials in SUP, windsurfing and other endurance events battled it out on the canals and waterways of the northern Dutch province of Friesland. A handful of celebrities who were invited to compete added spice to the event, as did the weather, which was wet, windy and uncomfortably cold.

The race proved successful enough to earn a re-run. And the following year's event was open to all comers, as a result of which 85 people competed. The format of this second race was also broadened to allow teams of two to five people to participate, allowing different individuals to tackle different stages. The changes increased the race's popularity and by 2012, when the number of competitors had jumped to 155, the 11-City SUP Tour had been further altered to allow people to complete single-day stages and not long afterwards allowances were made for people who were only able to compete on weekends.

In light of these developments, the introduction of the non-stop category was almost inevitable. Paddlers who elect to complete the course this way sacrifice the opportunity to enjoy some of its prime attractions. Those who opt out of the non-stop category enjoy the rural scenery of northern Holland, a panorama of forests and fields complete with cows, sheep and windmills, through which the route meanders. They also experience the beauty and culture of the 11 historic cities that form staging posts along the route. The 11-City SUP begins and ends in Leeuwarden, an old trading centre and the capital of Friesland. Subsequent stages along the route are at Sloten, Workum, Franeker and Dokkum. In each of the 11 cities competitors are issued with a SUP 11-City cross, a 'medal of honour' to prove that they have completed the entire 136 miles (220 km). In a novel touch, competitors can book to spend nights aboard authentic Frisian sailing ships at the end of each stage.

PROFILE

Born in 1974 in the Netherlands, at the age of 16 Anne-Marie Reichman discovered her passion for windsurfing. She subsequently competed on lakes across the country and, after leaving school, honed her skills in the North Sea surf on the west coast of Holland. Foreign competitions beckoned and over the next couple of years Reichman travelled to Denmark and Sweden and as far as South Africa and Hawaii. At Maui in 1997 she got to grips with big-wave conditions and the following year debuted in the PWA (Professional Windsurfers Association) World Cup. In 2003, a seasoned performer, she ranked in the top three on the PWA world championship list.

In autumn 2008, now a professional windsurfer and avid paddleboard enthusiast, and inspired by the resurgence of SUP in Hawaii, Reichman set out to paddle the route of what later became the 11-City. The route she had chosen was not something she dreamt up but rather a historical ice-skating path once taken by farmers in Friesland. It was mostly canals, which meant flat water, but the occasional torrid headwind, blowing up suddenly, could make life difficult. Punctuating Reichman's journey were the so-called 'Pearls of Friesland', the 11 cities dating back to the 1700s and beyond. Her 11-City Tour, which she completed in 38 hours, became the blueprint for what has since become a world-famous event. With the motto, 'Dream of life, live your dream', Reichman had laid the foundations of an event that would encourage others to follow their own personal stars.

STATISTICS

Inaugural non-stop division 2014:

 Competitors at start: 12

 Competitors at finish: 8

 Winner: Arnaud Frennet (Chile), 26 hours 20 minutes

 Winner of staged solo male race 2014: Bart de Zwart (Netherlands), 22 hours 6 minutes 39 seconds

 Number of times de Zwart has won: 4 (record)

DEVIZES TO WESTMINSTER INTERNATIONAL CANOE RACE (THE 'DW')

What is it? A non-stop canoe race that takes around 24 hours to finish

Location: England

Established: 1948

Held: Annually over the Easter Weekend

Equipment: Canoe, paddles, wetsuit and a support crew

Distance: 125 miles (201 km)

Obstacles: 76 locks and a 1,647-ft (502-m) tunnel that have to be portaged, steep and slippery banks, weirs, strong winds, pleasure craft and angry swans

Some might prefer to spend the Easter Weekend tucking into hot-cross buns and Easter eggs, but every year around 600 paddlers opt instead to enjoy the holiday in a small canoe travelling furiously along the canals and rivers that connect the sleepy Wiltshire market town of Devizes with the UK seat of government in Westminster.

In this race, competitors chose their own start time, so as to hit the tidal stretch of the River Thames at Teddington at the precise moment when the tide is turning. Get the timing wrong and it is virtually impossible to make any headway against the flood stream.

The origins of the race go back to a £5 bet struck in the Greyhound pub in Pewsey near Devizes, between drinkers discussing ways to get round a planned rail and bus strike in 1920. The initial challenge was to reach the sea at Mudeford, but in 1948 a new challenge was issued to see if it was possible to paddle from Devizes to the Houses of Parliament in London in under 100 hours.

In Easter 1948 four scouts took up the challenge and completed the run in 89 hours 50 minutes. Their exploits caught the attention of the national media and cinema showings in Devizes were interrupted to give updates on their progress.

Participants can enter in five classes: Senior Doubles (non-stop); Junior Doubles, for those aged between 15 and 19 (four stages with overnight stops); Senior Singles (four stages); Endeavour Class, run as a challenge aimed at those considering taking part in the non-stop competition (four stages); Vets/Juniors (for parents and their offspring to paddle together and bond).

Famous competitors have included Paddy Ashdown (for a Royal Marines crew) and Chay Blyth (for the Parachute Regiment).

PROFILE

The 2008 race didn't begin well for former Royal Navy training instructor Lee Menday as the organisers decided to delay the start until 4 p.m. on the Saturday, due to some of the worst ever weather conditions in the race's history. As an amputee, Lee would now have to negotiate more of the slippery portages in the dark without being able to see where he was placing his artificial leg.

Undaunted, he set off with his race partner Les Thompson, and between them they fought on despite suffering a fall at one portage, painful rubbing from his loose limb and a freezing cold stump. With food, drink and encouragement from their support crew, and a cup of tea from the flask of a sympathetic spectator, they persevered through the blizzards and bitter cold.

The pair had failed to complete the race on their only other attempt 12 years previously. Now older, less fit and minus one leg, they were determined to finish this time. They reached Teddington just on schedule and after the final 17.5 miles (28 km) of the tidal stretch of the Thames, they finished in a time of 26 hours 27 minutes.

STATISTICS

Fastest winning time: 15 hours 34 minutes 12 seconds, Tim Cornish and Brian Greenham (1979)

Approximate number of paddle strokes: 90,000

 Competitors in 2014: 635

 Average age of senior competitors: 40¼

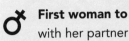 **First woman to compete:** Sheila Burnett (1971) with her partner Colin Dickens*

 First official sanctioned female crew to finish: M. Hossack and D. Johnson (1976) – 31 hours 6 minutes

 Percentage of female competitors in 2014: 20 per cent

£ **Cost of a racing kayak:** £500 (second-hand) to £3,000 and beyond

* Initially the race was deemed too arduous for women to enter and Burnett was one of the first women to compete using an assumed name; she and Dickens were later disqualified when the organisers found out Burnett was a woman.

ÖTILLÖ (ISLAND TO ISLAND)

What is it? A timed running and swimming race from island to island

Location: Sweden

Established: 2006

Held: Annually on first Monday in September

Equipment: Good teammate, triathlon wetsuit, shoes that remain comfortable and light when wet

Distance: 47 miles (75 km): 6 miles (10 km) swimming, 41 miles (65 km) running

Obstacles: 26 islands, a lot of water in between

An hour and a half from Stockholm, Sweden, is the Stockholm archipelago with dozens of peaceful islands covered in pine trees. The island of Utö was once a sleepy mining community and later a fashionable resort frequented by the likes of Greta Garbo and August Strindberg. The hotel Utö Värdshus has been owned by Anders Malm since 1997. In 2002 he and some of the staff, the Andersson brothers, were in the bar when they challenged one another: 'Last team of two to Sandhamn pays for hotel, dinner and drinks.'

The next morning, two teams of two set off on their route; their 'checkpoints' were three different restaurants on islands and the rule was that the team arriving second had to drink and pay for whatever the first team had ordered for them. Twenty-four hours later, they arrived at the finish – but too tired to party. It had gone so well they did the same thing the following year, and in 2006 it was developed by Michael Lemmel and Mats Skott, professional multi-sport athletes and pioneers in the Scandinavian adventure racing scene, into a commercial race.

The race now goes the other way around, starting beside the Seglarhotell in Sandhamn and finishing at Utö Värdshus on Utö, taking in the large islands of Runmarö, Nämdö and Ornö, as well as smaller ones. The course goes through forest, onto rocks, trails and gravelled roads, and in and out of the water over and over again, but there are high-quality food stations at restaurants along the way, in keeping with the race's history. Apparently the only way to succeed in the race is 'by not stopping, with constant movement' for the full 24 hours. Racers are advised to swim in trainers, wearing backpacks, and to run wearing thin triathlete wetsuits for fast transitions in and out of water.

The top teams in 2014 were from Sweden or other Scandinavian countries but competitors come from as far away as Mexico and Brunei, as well as Canada, Russia and all over Europe. Petter Askergren, Sweden's most famous rapper, teamed up with Jojje Borssen from *Runner's World* magazine in 2014 to inspire young people in Sweden to be more active. A local brewery provided a special ÖtillÖ beer for finishers and spectators. Mats and Jesper Andersson, two of the four who made the original challenge, have raced every year to date.

PROFILE

Another man who has competed every year is Jonas Colting, Swedish star endurance athlete and author of several books on health and lifestyle. In September 2008 he described the ÖtillÖ as a long, cold day 'with a lot of misery' in a wild and spectacular environment. He teamed up that year with 43-year-old Pasi Salonen, 20 years earlier a star of Swedish triathlon and national champion 'before succumbing to the demands of family and work. And eating ice cream.' Pasi started training again, lost 10 kg, and competed in the Swedish Ironman to prove that he was ready.

The two had attempted the ÖtillÖ in 2006 and 2007, and had promised they would never go back to its 'slippery rocks and really cold water'. The organisers had insisted on the wearing of flotation devices over your wetsuit for safety, which made swimming (and running) uncomfortable. But in 2008 the list of mandatory equipment was reduced. Jonas and Pasi decided to go 'minimalist' to aid with the fast transitions in and out of water that are the key to a quick race. They would carry everything they needed in a small fanny pack and swim in their shoes.

Although the rain held off on the day, it was a brutal race and Jonas wished he'd packed some ibuprofen. Pasi was having his own problems and Jonas had to stop and wait for him at times. That year, the organisers had included a bicycle stretch for one of the longer sections to allow more people to finish, and Jonas was handed a heavy tourist bike complete with a basket. Cycling along the road in wetsuits he said, 'We must have been quite a sight'.

As they closed in on the finish line in just over 10 hours, the team were gung-ho about completing first. 'We took the time to bask in the glory of not only winning but actually just finishing this monster.' He says the ÖtillÖ is different and more laid back than an Ironman, but certainly not easier. He has now won the race three times. In 2014, from 6 July to 15 August, he also swam 398 miles (640 km) across Sweden, from Stockholm on the east coast to Gothenburg on the west coast, through lakes, sea, canals and rivers, averaging 10.5 miles (17 km) per day through wind and waves and cold water, and raising over $100,000 for WaterAid.

STATISTICS

 Number of teams allowed to race: 115

 Length of each swim section: From 100–1,600 m (328–5,249 ft)

 Number of times racers go in and out of water: 40+

Water temperature: 10–16°C

Number of teams that entered in 2006: 11

THE WORLD'S TOUGHEST RACES

 Number of teams that completed within the time limit in 2006: 2

 Course record: 8 hours 16 minutes 12 seconds, set by Team Milebreaker (2014)

 Women's course record: 10 hours 26 minutes 31 seconds, set by team Puppt TS-MAD (2014)

 Winning team 2014: Swedish Armed Forces

SWIMMING THE ENGLISH CHANNEL

What is it? A swim across one of the world's busiest shipping lanes

Location: From Dover, England, to Calais, France

Established: 1875

Held: Any time during the 'Channel-swimming season', usually between late June and early September

Equipment: Swimming costume, goggles, swimming hat, light sticks, sun cream, support vessel, and a special mix of petroleum jelly and lanolin (goose fat is so nineteenth century)

Distance: 21 miles (34 km) (but only in the unlikely event that there are no tides)

Obstacles: Force 6 gales, 2 m-high waves, jellyfish, seaweed and oil tankers

In 1873, merchant seaman Captain Matthew Webb read an account of a failed attempt to swim across the English Channel. Racing swimmer J. B. Johnson had tried to make the crossing from England to France but was forced to abandon his swim just over an hour into the trip, as the cold conditions cut off the circulation in his legs. Webb had learnt to swim as a boy in the strong currents of the River Severn and had even been awarded £100 for diving into the ocean to try to rescue a fellow mariner who had fallen overboard. He decided to see if he could succeed where Johnson had failed.

He quit his job and began an intensive training schedule at Lambeth Baths in London and in the River Thames. His first attempt to swim the Channel in August 1875 was brought to a halt by a violent storm, but 12 days later he managed the crossing in just under 22 hours – in spite of being stung by a jellyfish and fighting against the tides.

Today the Channel Swimming Association verifies attempts to repeat Webb's feat of endurance, and co-ordinates the pilots and support vessels that accompany swimmers to help them navigate across the busy shipping lanes on the way to France. The rules are that you have to make the crossing in a standard swimming costume, i.e. one 'not offering thermal protection or buoyancy'. Most swimmers opt for a liberal coating of grease in an attempt to keep warm and combat chaffing. You can have food and drink passed to you throughout the journey but any direct contact with the support vessel and your challenge is over. If you manage to keep going, you could be in Calais and in the record books after somewhere between 7 and 27 hours.

PROFILE

Brojen Das became the first Asian swimmer to cross the Channel. In Bangladesh, the word 'brojen' means 'king of the heavens', but from 1960 to 1974 he also became King of the Channel, the title awarded to the person who has made the most crossings at any given time.

As a young boy, Brojen swam in the turbulent waters of the Buriganga River, which flows past the city of Dhaka.

He became a national champion swimmer in Bangladesh, known as East Pakistan until 1971, but was overlooked by the selectors for the Pakistan Olympic squad in favour of four swimmers from West Pakistan. He switched to long-distance sea swimming and was invited to take part in the Billy Butlins-sponsored Channel swimming competition in 1958. Thirty swimmers entered the competition but only nine completed the crossing, with Brojen finishing in first place. Over the next two years he completed a further five crossings, the fastest of which was in September 1960 which he managed in 10 hours 39 minutes. He died in 1998 at the age of 71 and his ashes were scattered in the Buriganga, where he had swum as a boy all those years before.

STATISTICS

 Fastest woman (England to France): Penny Lee Dean, 7 hours 40 minutes (1978)

 Fastest man (England to France): Chad Hundeby, 7 hours 17 minutes (1994)

 Earliest swim in the season: 29 May – Kevin Murphy (1990)

 Latest swim in the season: 28 October – Michael Read (1979)

THE WORLD'S TOUGHEST RACES

 Oldest swimmer: Clifford Batt – 67 years, 240 days (1987)

 Youngest swimmer: Thomas Gregory – 11 years, 330 days (1988)

 Fastest backstroke: Tina Neill, 13 hours 22 minutes (2005)

 Fastest butterfly: Julie Bradshaw, 14 hours 18 minutes (2002)

CADIZ FREEDOM SWIM

What is it? Extreme open-water swimming race

Location: Cape Town, South Africa

Established: 2001

Held: Annually on Freedom Day, 27 April (or the closest date possible, dependent on weather conditions)

Equipment: Standard swimming costume and official cap; grease and goggles are permitted

Distance: 4.7 miles (7.5 km)

Obstacles: Cold water, great white sharks

The Cadiz Freedom Swim from the beach at Murray's Bay on Robben Island to the beach in Big Bay, Bloubergstrand, commemorates the date of the first democratic elections in South Africa in 1994, when Nelson Mandela was elected President and the apartheid era came to an end. Robben Island, now a UNESCO World Heritage Site, was the prison for political prisoners and freedom fighters against apartheid.

Back in 1909, Henry Charteris Hooper swam from Robben Island to the old harbour of Cape Town, a distance of 7 miles (11 km) which took him almost seven hours. Astonishingly, the 4.7-mile (7.5-km) swim to Bloubergstrand, the route of the current race, has been completed in just over 1 hour 33 minutes (2005 record). I suppose you wouldn't want to hang about with those sharks nearby.

It is recognised as one of the world's most extreme sea races, with unpredictable weather conditions, and solo swimmers must pass the qualifications specified in the rules and regulations. The Atlantic Ocean is a challenging environment, with a risk of hypothermia. All swimmers must be accompanied by a motorised vessel for safety; two swimmers may use the same support boat, provided neither is ever more than 10 m away from it, so they should swim at the same pace, and it is possible for experienced participants to use a paddle rather than motorised support boat. There is also a relay race that takes place around the southern rocks at Big Bay, where teams swim loops and there is no need for support.

The organisers may cancel the swim if the ocean swell makes swimming unsafe, if the wind is too strong or visibility too poor for support boats, or if there are clear sightings of sharks in the area. It is the responsibility of swimmers to ensure they are capable of swimming if the water temperature is low.

Swimmers include South African and international athletes. The 2011 race was won by renowned Bulgarian marathon swimmer Petar Stoychev, former world-record holder for the fastest English Channel swim.

PROFILE

South African former businessman and open-water swimmer Ram Barkai began sponsoring the current annual event in 2007, for the benefit of Vista Nova School for children with learning difficulties in the Western Cape. There is now a Freedom Swim Series of cold-water races around the Cape, organised with the aim of promoting swimming and raising funds for good causes. The swims take place on public holidays, celebrating important days in South Africa's history.

Barkai, born in 1957 in Israel, specialises in extreme cold-water swimming and holds the record for the world's most southerly swim in Antarctica. He and four swimming mates formed the International Ice Swimming Association in 2009, to promote safe swimming in icy waters around the world. It introduced the Ice Mile as the ultimate achievement: one mile swum in water of 5°C or lower, wearing a standard costume, cap and goggles.

STATISTICS

Water temperature average: 13–14°C

Record for most crossings: 55 times, Theodore Yach

Age of youngest finisher: 12

Age of oldest finisher: 65

Number of competitors annually: Approx. 500

Relay teams must comprise: 4 swimmers

Relay teams swim: 8 loops of approx. 0.7 miles (1.15 km); total 5.7 miles/9.2 km

DUSI CANOE MARATHON

What is it? Biggest canoeing event on African continent

Location: Pietermaritzburg to Durban, KwaZulu-Natal, east coast of South Africa

Established: 1951

Held: Annually in mid-February

Equipment: Hydration gear and fluids; normal marathon K1/K2/K3 of robust construction with overstern rudder; splash cover; lifejacket; helmet required in the case of very full river conditions

Distance: Approx. 75 miles (120 km) in three stages

Obstacles: Temperatures exceeding 40°C, rocky river, portages of up to 2.5 miles (4 km)

This big South African canoe race is held in mid-February to take advantage of summer rainfalls. Paddlers must have completed qualifying races and prove proficiency, physical condition and experience on Grade 2 rivers – this is not a race for novices.

It starts on the Umsindusi River running through Pietermaritzburg, with several weirs as well as rapids using water released from the Henley Dam. Around the halfway stage of the race, the Umsindusi meets the larger Umgeni and the challenges increase with Grade 3+ rapids. Portaging is allowed on the large rapids, and is in fact necessary in places, but that's not really an easy option when it means carrying your craft over steep hills and through thick bush for up to 2.5 miles (4 km). Safety marshalls and divers are stationed at some major rapids and obstacles, but it is up to the paddlers themselves to determine the safest route. The website is full of information on the routes and even has tips about the best way to tackle particular spots.

Camping and local accommodation are available at the two overnight stops. Finishers all receive a Dusi medal.

The idea began back in the Second World War when a young Ian Player from Johannesburg, serving with the South African Armoured Division in Italy, was feeling homesick as he sat by a campfire. Later to become a great conservationist and already passionate about the cause, he came up with the idea of a Pietermaritzburg to Durban river race initially to draw attention to the need for wildlife protection in his homeland. He first tried it in 1950 but had to give up halfway. Then he attempted it again with seven other paddlers in December 1951, but the race was dogged by days of low rivers followed by a flash flood. Player got a night adder bite and his partner quit on Christmas Eve. Player was the only one to reach Durban, 'bedraggled and exhausted' – but he'd done the Dusi. He won the next two races. By 1956, 48 paddlers were competing and the overnight stops were introduced. The race continued to evolve over the years, topping 100 racers in 1967. By the millennium year, there were 2,217 paddlers doing the Dusi.

After winning the 2014 Dusi with partner Andy Birkett, Sbonelo Zondi teamed up with Hank McGregor two weeks later and emerged victorious in the Non-Stop Dusi, otherwise known as 'Dusi in a day', a one-day version of the canoe marathon, which takes a similar route.

PROFILE

The 60th anniversary Dusi race in 2011 was a tribute to the 'Dusi King' Graeme Pope-Ellis, who had completed 46 Dusis.

The Dusi King, whose Dusi career spanned 45 years, was born and raised on a farm on the banks of the river. He entered his first Dusi Canoe Marathon in 1965 at the age of 17, while a student in Pietermaritzburg. He first won the race in 1972 with K2 partner Eric Clarke. Over the next two decades he won 15 titles (K1 and K2). Five of the wins were with Peter Peacock, with whom he won every race from 1975 to 1980. Then he became the first man to win it solo in 1981. At the age of 38, he won the marathon and broke his own record of 10 years earlier.

One thing that gave him an edge was his knowledge of the river, as well as his stamina for the long portages that are critical to the outcome of the race. He passed his knowledge on to other paddlers, mentoring Martin Dreyer and former world champion Shaun Rubenstein.

He was killed tragically in a farming accident in late 2010, having completed every edition of the three-day race from 1965.

STATISTICS

Attracts between: 1,600–2,000 competitors a year

Stage one: 26 miles (42 km)

WATER

Stage two: 28.5 miles (46 km)

Stage three: 22 miles (36 km)

 Ian Player's time on 22 December 1951: 6 days 8 hours 15 minutes

 2014 winning team: A. J. Birkett and S. Zondi, 7 days 43 hours 50 minutes

NATIONAL FIERLJEPPEN MANIFESTATION

What is it? Canal jumping

Location: Friesland, Netherlands

Established: 1771

Held: Annually in August

Equipment: Long pole (*polsstok*)

Distance: As far as possible

Obstacles: Body of water such as river or canal

If pole-vaulting seems to you a little tame, perhaps the more extreme Dutch version of *fierljeppen* or 'far leaping' across canals will appeal.

One legend has it that canal jumping originated in Holland when poachers used to vault over canals when stealing eggs from farmers. Others deny that a national sport could have such base origins, suggesting it may have simply developed as a method of quickly crossing the extensive waterways between fields. Besides, can you imagine doing this while carrying eggs?

Athletes dig an aluminium pole or *polsstok* into the bank of a canal, and sprint and then leap on to it in the hope that the momentum will carry them across the muddy water; vaulters shimmy to the top of the pole in order to land as far away as possible (ensuring at least they clear the water) in a sandpit on the other side. The pole, which has a flat plate at the bottom to prevent it from sinking into mud, gathers speed as it falls so vaulters find themselves crashing to land fairly swiftly.

The National Fierljeppen Manifestation is an annual contest and, unlike pole-vaulting where the aim is to go high, competitors endeavour to vault the greatest distance. Most participants go barefoot or wear trainers, but bicycle inner tubes strapped to the feet are also allowed and some find they provide good traction.

Although records of canal-leaping go back to the eighteenth century and it enjoyed a revival after the Second World War, it has only come back into fashion in recent years, with the number of competitions increasing, and although it is part of Dutch culture and learnt at a young age, not everyone is at national level. In local competitions, many canal-leapers lose their grip on the pole and fall into the water, which probably makes it quite a good spectator sport. It is traditionally a summer sport.

PROFILE

Bart Helmholt's 2014 record of 70 ft 8 in (21.55 m) gets him first place in the all-time top 50 since records began in the 1970s (Jaco de Groot is in second place with 69 ft 8 in/21.25 m). The native of Friesland, born in 1982, has recorded 1,615 jumps.

During one tournament, a man lost his false teeth during his far leaping. He found them in the sand, dusted them off and put them back in again.

Moves to avoid if you try the sport include landing with the pole between your legs.

The official rankings site lists records for almost 600 active jumpers.

The sport has been emulated on US television – as 'ditch-vaulting' on *The Amazing Race* – and on the Japanese reality TV show *Sasuke* (also known as Ninja Warrior).

STATISTICS

 Height of pole: 3–13 m, depending on width of canal

The records for 2014:

 Men: Bart Helmholt (Dutch and Frisian records) – 70 ft 8 in (21.55 m)

 Women: Dymphie van Rooijen (Dutch and Holland records) – 55 ft 6 in (16.91 m)

 Juniors (under 20): shared between Jaco de Groot and Age Hulder – 67 ft (20.41 m)

 Youth (under 16): Age Hulder – 63 ft 1 in (19.24 m)

Veterans: Theo van Kooten – 67 ft 7in (20.60 m)

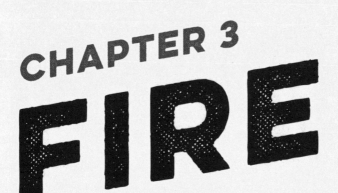

CHAPTER 3

FIRE

COSTA RICA COASTAL CHALLENGE

What is it? Jungle, trail and alpine six-day stage race run along tropical Pacific coastline

Location: South-west Costa Rica

Established: 2004

Held: Annually January–February

Equipment: Camping gear, hydration and emergency gear, lockable storage bin

Distance: 124–155 miles (200–250 km) depending on the year's route

Obstacles: Mountains, rainforest, beaches, river estuaries

The Costa Rica Coastal Challenge, otherwise known as the Coastal Challenge Rainforest Run, is an ultra run spread over six days, ending near the border of Panama in a remote fishing village. It takes athletes down sandy beaches and across river estuaries, also weaving in and out of the Talamanca mountain range, and over ridges and highlands to make it an assault course of topography. Competitors run along dirt tracks, rocky ravines and mountain trails, over ridgelines, past reefs and waterfalls and through jungle and cloud forest, entering one of the world's premier rainforests at Corcovado National Park, a UNESCO World Heritage Site. The view changes from vivid-green forest and fields to deep-blue ocean.

Like the Marathon des Sables (see page 76), the Coastal Challenge is a multi-stage race over six days but you are not required to carry all your gear, allowing you to run light and fast. You carry only water; food is provided and luggage transported to camps each night. The Coastal Challenge also offers a choice of the longer Expedition category (around 147 miles/236 km) for experienced runners or the shorter Adventure category (78 miles/125 km). This makes it a truly open event, encouraging all individuals to fulfil their dreams and develop their potential. Cut-off times keep the level of competition high in the Expedition category; people who slow down risk being relegated to the Adventure category.

But 'the run is only part of the challenge', and it's not for softies according to Costa Rican adventure racer Rodrigo Carazo, who wanted to create an event through some of the most inaccessible parts of the country. It can be as hot as the Sahara and has punishing tropical humidity. Rain is not uncommon later in the day. The sound of runners scares away most snakes.

Though routes change every year (but are made public before the event starts), every effort is made to avoid roads and focus on unexpected, varied and rugged terrain, often in the middle of nowhere. The race finishes with a 'victory loop' to Drakes Bay for a day on the beach, an awards ceremony and a closing party at an isolated village.

PROFILE

Andrea Minarcek wrote in a blog for *National Geographic* that by day four of the Coastal Challenge Rainforest Run in 2009, the temperature was already in the low thirties by 8 a.m. and most people's feet were covered in blisters. After hiking for an hour, they came to an almost vertical track climbing 3,000 ft (914 m) in a mile and a half through the jungle, and some of the racers started to struggle. It was then that she witnessed some of the spirit that makes the challenge special.

Robyn Benincasa, born in New York and brought up in Arizona, competed at state and national level in gymnastics, diving and cross-country in her youth. She graduated in marketing, but after being bitten by the adventure-racing bug gave up her 'high heels' job and became a full-time San Diego firefighter, and world champion adventure racer and ironman competitor. She has been featured in Sports Illustrated, the New York Times and Vogue as well as outdoors adventure publications. In her spare time she delivers team-building talks.

In 2007, however, Benincasa had undergone resurfacing surgery on her right hip and the future of her adventure racing looked uncertain. Undaunted, she decided to launch Project Athena with a team of other female outdoor athletes. Project Athena's goal is to help survivors of breast cancer or other medical conditions to achieve their athletic goals.

Benincasa was racing the Coastal Challenge with Team Project Athena that day at the age of 42. When she saw one of her teammates struggling, she strapped her onto a towline on her backpack and pulled her up the hill. Minarcek quoted her as saying, 'It just feels so good to know I'm back up and running!'

STATISTICS

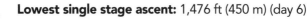 **Total elevation gain:** 34,000+ ft (10,363 m)

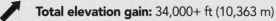 **Longest single stage in 2013:** 33 miles (52.5 km) (day 3)

 Highest single stage ascent: 9,678 ft (2,950 m) (day 4)

 Lowest single stage ascent: 1,476 ft (450 m) (day 6)

 Number of competitors in 2005: 63

 Distance between aid stations (for fruit, water, snacks): 7.5–11 miles (12–18 km)

 **Length of route in 2014:** 140 miles (225 km)

 Winner 2014 Expedition category, male: Mike Wardian, USA (23 hours 26 minutes 23 seconds)

 Time differential between winner and second place, male: 25 minutes 32 seconds

 Winner 2014 Expedition category, female: Jo Meek, UK (29 hours 17 minutes 19 seconds)

 Time differential between winner and second place, female: 57 minutes 2 seconds

 Nationalities finishing in top 10 male and female 2014: USA, Spain, Germany, France, Chile, Costa Rica, Australia, Italy, Portugal

TOUR D'AFRIQUE

What is it? Four-month-long mountain-bike race down the entire length of Africa

Location: From Cairo to Cape Town

Established: 2003

Held: Annually from January to May

Equipment: Bike, tent, spare parts

Distance: 7,456 miles (12,000 km)

Obstacles: Deserts, rugged mountain climbs, dirt roads, stifling heat, infections

Dubbed 'a test of mind, body and bicycle', this trans-continental expedition covers 10 countries, from the ancient temples of the Nile via the Sudanese desert to cross the Equator in Kenya, passing Victoria Falls and the Kalahari and Namib deserts, before arriving in Cape Town in the shadow of Table Mountain.

The inaugural Tour d'Afrique established the Guinness World Record for the fastest human-powered crossing of Africa. Fortunately the race today is divided into timed stages, with days off for you to stop and explore. You can sign up for the expedition category only, if you think the sheer distance and terrain are enough of a challenge, or sign up for a limited number of race sections or time trials. For those who take on the full four-month Tour d'Afrique, the commitment is huge.

What better way to see the jewels of Africa than from the saddle of a bike – approaching Mount Kilimanjaro on a lava rock road through the desert, for example, or pedalling into safari country in Tanzania? While taking in some of the continent's best-known sights, the tour gives riders an opportunity to experience the real Africa: riding alongside farmers around Lake Malawi, or finding your way blocked by an elephant in Botswana. As cycling adventures go, it's one of a lifetime.

Trucks carry most of your gear, which you pack up into a small locker every morning. Accommodation is all camping, with basic facilities. The cost? A whopping US$14,900 for the whole Tour d'Afrique, although shorter sections are available. Still, this is no ordinary camping trip. With all planning and organisation taken care of, participants are free to enjoy the wide variety of cultures and landscapes, and to use skill and stamina to finish as fast as possible in perhaps the longest and toughest cycle race in the world.

PROFILE

Erin, who did the Tour d'Afrique in 2010, joked about how she used to call hot summer days in New York 'Africa-hot'. Once she'd cycled through Malawi, she realised 'it's only Africa-hot in Africa'. The intense humidity and baking temperatures caused her to sweat at the slightest movement: 'You need a shower by the time you… unzip your tent.' Malawi was also a danger zone for malaria and other tropical infections – any scratches or bug bites could get infected overnight and require a course of antibiotics. On the first full day in the country, they had to cycle 75 miles (120 km) against a headwind in these conditions. Camping by the blue waters of Lake Malawi sounds like a perfect way to cool off, until you consider the possibility of organ-attacking parasites. Better, Erin decided, to cool off with a beer at the beach bar.

While passing through the Muslim country of Sudan earlier, she'd had to cover up out of respect, which provided another challenge when it came to beating the heat. But it was also in Sudan, two weeks into the adventure, that she started to understand the real value of doing an expedition like the Tour d'Afrique, beyond simply testing herself as a cyclist.

The first hour or two of each day were typically exhausting, even before they left camp: taking down tents, applying sun cream, checking the bike, packing up all the kit. The end of the day brought relief from riding the bike, but might also involve hand-washing your entire wardrobe. To this woman who had formerly worked at a New York financial firm and considered herself independent, it was a revelation to find that washing and cooking and riding extreme distances daily with absolutely no modern conveniences was true independence and self-sufficiency. And with that came an appreciation of help from others when it was offered, and a joy in the simple things she was able to improvise, such as a shower under a garden hose.

Erin also raised an impressive amount of money for African charities along the way. After returning home after the four-month ride through Africa, she would miss 'the luxury of challenge, purpose, accomplishment and camaraderie' that every day brought.

STATISTICS

 Days of riding: 94

 Days of rest: 27

 Average daily distance: 78 miles (125 km)

 2014 fastest man: David Grosshans (Australia), 384 hours

 2014 fastest woman: Ina de Visser (Netherlands), 386 hours

 2013 fastest man: Pascal Duquette (Canada), 325 hours

 2013 fastest woman: Bridget O'Meara (South Africa), 413 hours

 Number of people who have participated in Tour d'Afrique trans-continental rides in Africa and elsewhere: 800

 Number of bicycles donated to healthcare and community development workers in Africa and India by Tour d'Afrique and their clients: 2,000

MARATHON DES SABLES

What is it? Ultramarathon foot race in six stages over seven days

Location: Morocco

Established: 1986

Held: Annually in April

Equipment: Solid, comfortable shoes, sun-protective clothing, hat, rucksack for food and drink

Distance: 150–156 miles (241–254 km)

Obstacles: Rough, stony ground, sandhills, temperatures in excess of 38°C, the occasional sand storm

In 1984 a French concert promoter named Frederick Bauer decided to go for a walk. Carrying everything he needed in a rucksack on his back, he set out to trek 200 miles (322 km) through what is generally regarded as one of the toughest and least-friendly environments on earth – the Sahara Desert.

Somewhere along the way Bauer had an idea. It wasn't enough that he was enjoying marching up and down sand dunes, battling sandstorms and frying his brains in the withering Sahara sun. Rather, what he decided was that he would like to help other, presumably like-minded souls get to grips with the desert and fry their brains too. It took him two more years to organise sponsors and iron out details about the course and other essential things. Finally, however, in 1986, the Marathon des Sables was born.

Entry in the race is expensive. Yet it could be argued that you get a lot of bang for your buck. For a start, there's the striking desert landscape. Then there's the behind-the-scenes organisation which makes the Marathon des Sables resemble the greatest show on earth. A legion of volunteers and support staff are deployed to ensure that everything runs smoothly. On hand, too, presumably to ensure that nobody becomes lost or falls ill and dies, is everything from thousands of litres of mineral water to a small hospital's worth of bandages and first aid gear to 100 all-terrain vehicles, a 52-strong medical team, two 'Ecureuil' helicopters and a Cessna plane.

If that's not enough, there's also a quartet of camels, a quintet of cameras, one editing bus, 23 other buses whose purpose isn't specified, an incinerator lorry for burning waste, one satellite image station, six satellite telephones and, finally, 15 computers with fax and Internet. Oh, and 6,000 painkillers, just in case. Indeed the Sahara has never looked so well equipped.

To keep things interesting, routes and formats change every year, and are not revealed until just before the race starts. There is a rest day after the longest stage, which might be very long indeed, up to 55 miles (91 km). Multi-bunk tents are provided, should runners wish to sleep at any stage. According to the website, the time runners spend in the tents, together with the challenges they face in the race, helps them to make friends for life.

PROFILE

With over 1,000 runners competing every year, and all the precautions taken, it is virtually impossible nowadays to become lost in the Marathon des Sables. However, circumstances were far different back in 1994 when the 39-year-old Italian runner and former Olympic pentathlete Mauro Prosperi became lost in a sandstorm. Initially, Prosperi wasn't alarmed; with the storm only abating at nightfall, his plan was to spend the night among the dunes and continue the next morning. He awoke and found, to his considerable surprise, the landscape completely transformed.

The first thing he did upon realising that he was lost was urinate into his water bottle. As the race was self supporting, he had food and sleeping gear but water, which was dispensed at checkpoints, was a major problem. Even so, he continued his progress, walking only during the cooler hours of the day and taking shelter from the sun the rest of the time. On the second day a helicopter flew over him, so close he could see the pilot's helmet. However, it flew away again after failing to see the flare that Prosperi fired.

The second setback came at a Muslim marabout, or shrine, when an aeroplane flew by but failed to see him on account of another sandstorm. After having survived on the blood of bats he had found in the roof, killed and consumed raw, Prosperi became convinced he was going to die. In what he claims was a calculated decision, designed to ensure that his body was found and his wife would therefore receive his policeman's pension, he lay down and slashed his wrists and waited for the inevitable. But his blood had thickened and wouldn't drain.

Prosperi took it as a sign. Determined to survive, he followed the advice the Tuareg had given to the runners before the race. This was to set their bearings by the clouds they saw on the horizon at dawn. Though the clouds would disappear during the day, the tribesmen said, in that direction lay life.

Prosperi became a 'man of the desert', surviving on snakes and lizards and plants he found in dry waterbeds. On the eighth day he came upon an oasis, where he drank, and saw a human footprint. The next day the sight of goats led him to a Berber encampment. The men were away at market, but the women cared for him, giving him goat's milk to drink and sending someone for the police.

It turned out that Prosperi had crossed the border into Algeria and was 181 miles (291 km) off course. In the ten days he'd been wandering in the desert he'd lost 16 kg. It took him two years to recover from his experience, but four years later he returned to the Marathon des Sables. It was not only the sense of unfinished business that brought him back – he had also fallen in love with the desert.

STATISTICS

 Number of competitors in each race: 1,000

 Fastest male time: 18 hours 59 minutes by Mohamad Ahansal (2013)

 Fastest female time: 24 hours 42 minutes by Meghan Hicks (2013)

 The youngest competitor ever to compete: 16

 The oldest competitor ever to compete: 79

 The average maximum speed of athletes: 14 km/hr

JUNGLE MARATHON

What is it? Foot race with swamps, river crossings and dense jungle canopy

Location: Near Santarém, Pará, Brazil

Established: 2004

Held: Annually in early October

Equipment: Totally self-sufficient except that cold and hot water are supplied, so bring dehydrated food for race and pre-race days; local currency to buy fresh food from villagers; hammock with mosquito net and rain sheet (full list of mandatory kit on website)

Distance: Choose from marathon (26.2 miles/42 km), four-stage (79 miles/127 km) or six-stage (158 miles/254 km)

Obstacles: 99 per cent humidity, possibility of meeting caiman or piranha while crossing rivers, or anaconda in the swamps, steep, muddy climbs

The Brazil Jungle Marathon, once voted by CNN as the 'world's toughest endurance race', is an extreme foot race that takes competitors through Flona Tapajós in areas of dense canopy without a chink of daylight, and through rivers populated by caiman and piranha. It's a self-supported race of relentless ups and downs in tall Amazon rainforest over six days. The race is open to anyone over 18 with a sense of adventure, but organisers advise newcomers not to take on the full six-stage race – which is like running five and a half marathons in six days – first time around. Temperatures reach close to 40°C but it's the 99 per cent humidity that makes it worse.

A 10–12-hour boat journey takes participants from the hamlet of Alter do Chao into the jungle, stopping for a swim break at a beach on the Tapajós river, where you may meet dolphins. At base camp there's a kit check and *bombeiros* (military firemen) give instruction on jungle safety, including poisonous flora and fauna to avoid; medics advise on how to avoid dehydration and heat exhaustion and there's even a foot-care expert to brief you on how to keep problems to a minimum, as racers will have wet feet for most of the course. At the first two checkpoints there's a compulsory 15-minute rest break to help with acclimatisation.

Locals prepare the routes and *bombeiros* sweep the route for dangers, keeping safety a priority. The course changes slightly every year. Because of the sensitive environment, the route is marked with biodegradable tape; camps have very basic jungle loos and showers. In some parts, villagers carry water on their heads for 3.7 miles (6 km) to the checkpoints. Medals and trophies are handmade by a Brazilian craftsman.

Large iguanas can be seen in the rivers, and swimmers are advised to shuffle their feet when entering the water because of stingrays. In the forest are monkeys, birds, butterflies and of course plenty of insects. Though most animals are likely to remain out of sight, wet weather can bring out snakes. Every year two or three runners spot a jaguar, and many report hearing them at night.

JUNGLE ULTRA

A similarly named event on the calendar, confusing things a little, is the Jungle Ultra, another stage race held in the Amazon jungle. This one is organised by Beyond the Ultimate as part of their four-part series (Jungle Ultra, Ice Ultra, Desert Ultra and Mountain Ultra), set up in 2012 by Wes Crutcher from Bournemouth, England, after he participated in the Jungle Marathon.

The Jungle Ultra is a race of a similar length that takes place in Manú National Park in Peru. A four-hour drive from Cuzco, Manú National Park is a biosphere reserve which ranges from the cloud forest of the Andes down into the Amazon rainforest. It starts at 10,500 ft (3,200 m) where the lack of oxygen is the first obstacle, and continues through 143 miles (230 km) of jungle trails including 70 river crossings. You carry your own hammock, food and kit. The chance of finishing is rated at 80 per cent.

Daniel Rowland won the 2014 Jungle Ultra in a time of 27 hours, and particularly loved the finish in the village of Pilcopata, where local children ran with him to the finish line amid crowds of people. For him, it was the opportunity to see a fascinating and remote part of the planet, as well as the character-building challenges of the event, that made the experience of a foot race in the jungle – 'as long as you don't mind being wet for a week'.

STATISTICS: 2014

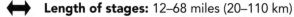 **Litres of water distributed to checkpoints:** 17,000

 Medical team members: 17

Number of staff: 200

Age of competitors: 18–70

 **Distance between checkpoints:** 3–6 miles (5–10 km)

Length of stages: 12–68 miles (20–110 km)

Number of participants: 50–60 from all over the world; limited to 75 to reduce impact on environment

 Fastest man: Grego Widdy (Guadeloupe), 46 hours 2 minutes

 Fastest woman (placed seventh overall): Benson Josie (England), 61 hours 7 minutes

SPARTATHLON

What is it? Ultramarathon

Location: Central and southern Greece

Established: 1983

Held: Annually in September

Equipment: Running gear

Distance: 153 miles (246 km)

Obstacles: Extreme heat, high humidity, cold nights, undulating and, at times, mountainous terrain, and uncompromising cut-off times

Described as 'the world's most gruelling road race', the Spartathlon has its origins in the epic history of ancient Greece. In 490 BC, on the eve of the Battle of Marathon, a runner named Pheidippides was dispatched from Athens to Sparta with the task of securing help in the upcoming struggle against the invading Persians. According the historian Herodotus, who records the story, Pheidippides arrived in Sparta the day after he set out.

For centuries, people believed that the tale was an exaggeration on the part of a historian whose reputation for veracity has been questioned over the years. But then, in 1982, an English Air Force Officer and classical enthusiast named John Foden led a team of fellow officers in a run from Athens to Sparta to see if the feat could be accomplished. To general surprise, Foden arrived in Sparta 37 hours 37 minutes after setting out, while fellow runner John Scholtens managed the trip in a mere 34 hours 30 minutes. After thousands of years, the story of Pheidippides' run had been confirmed.

This heralded the beginning of the Spartathlon, which combines the romantic appeal of ancient Greece with the most rigorous standards of Ultramarathon running. Beginning in pre-dawn darkness beneath the ancient acropolis in Athens, the run encompasses some of the most famous place names in antiquity. Much has changed since then, of course, and in the beginning of the race particularly the industrial sprawl of modern Athens can leave competitors dismayed. Redemption comes with the appearance of the sparkling waters of the Saronic Gulf, with the island of Salamis floating idyllically offshore while inland mountains of craggy grey limestone pile up. After the momentous crossing of the Corinth canal and passing through the evocative ruins of ancient Corinth, the course leads through the rolling countryside of Nemea, legendary home of the Lion that Heracles conquered in one of his mighty labours, where vineyards sit side by side with orchards and olive groves.

Shortly afterwards, runners reach what is, quite literally, the high point of the race. This is the ascent (and subsequent descent) of the 3,600-ft (1,100-m) Mount Parthenio, a challenge which occurs 'in the dead of night'. The difficulty is heightened by the lack of a decent path. Legend has it that it was here Pheidippides encountered the god Pan, which modern observers have conjectured might have been a case of the same fatigue-induced hallucinations that afflict modern runners.

It's no wonder that the Spartathlon attracts the world's best long-distance runners, over 300 of whom are invited every year to participate after a rigorous selection process. It's no surprise, either, that most years the majority of them fail to reach Sparta, knocked out by high heat and humidity, tough terrain, the sheer distance of the race and gruelling cut-off points. Those who do manage the distance get to kiss the foot of the vast bronze statue of Leonidas, legendary hero of Thermopylae who, when the invading Persians demanded that he and his men lay down their arms, reputedly said, 'Come and get them.'

The race adheres to the notion of Olympic purity and offers no other rewards apart from a laurel crown, a cup of water from the Evrotas river and the passion, enthusiasm and hospitality of the modern Greek people.

PROFILE

No record of the Spartathlon would be complete without mention of legendary athlete and modern renaissance man Yiannis Kouros. A poet and musician, Kouros' four Spartathlons have netted him not only four wins but also the four fastest times ever recorded. His world record time of 20 hours 25 minutes was set in the second ever Spartathlon in 1984, but it was his performance in 1983's inaugural race that had fellow athletes talking.

He and another athlete, a well-known English runner, had missed the application deadline but officials asked the original group of world-class triathletes if the pair might be accepted as last-minute inclusions. The athletes agreed mainly on behalf of the Englishman. When subsequently the then unknown Kouros went on to win the race in the incredible time of 20 hours 29 minutes 4 seconds, coming in 3 hours 15 minutes ahead of the next competitor, conspiracy theories abounded with talk of runners getting lifts in cars under the cover of darkness. Englishman Alex Fairbrother, who placed third in the race, was openly sceptical. Kouros, he declared, did not 'have the experience or class to get anywhere near Dave Dowdle's 170-mile (274-km) world track best over a good flat surface in good climactic conditions.'

Kouros proved himself with an emphatic win in a multi-day stage race along the Danube in April of the following year, which was followed by his world-record effort in the Spartathlon in September. Since then he has continued to win races and break records with astonishing regularity. In 2005, further inspired by the Pheidippides legend, he ran from Athens to Sparta and all the way back to Athens again. Kouros puts his success down to the power of the mind. 'When other people get tired they stop. I don't,' he claims. 'I take over my body with my mind. I tell it that it's not tired and it listens.'

STATISTICS

 Course record: 20 hours 25 minutes set by Yiannis Kouros (1984)

 Second fastest time: 22 hours 20 minutes 1 second set by three-time American winner Scott Jurek (2008)

Fastest female time: 26 hours 53 minutes 40 seconds set by Szilvia Lubics of Hungary

 Second fastest female time: 27 hours 2 minutes 10 seconds set by Elizabeth Hawker (2012)

 Pheidippides died of exhaustion upon completing his exploit

ATACAMA CROSSING

What is it? Six-stage running race across the world's driest desert

Location: Chile

Established: 2004

Held: Annually (month varies)

Equipment: Backpack, camping and cooking gear, clothes for heat and cold, food

Distance: 155 miles (250 km)

Obstacles: Sand dunes, packed earth, river crossings, salt flats, gravel and relentless sun

West of the Andes, the Atacama Desert is the driest place on earth, 50 times drier than California's Death Valley – one of the few deserts on Earth that receives absolutely no rain – and its lunar landscape is used by NASA to test planetary rover vehicles. Because it is so arid, some of the world's oldest mummies have been found in the Atacama, dating back 7,000 years. The Atacama Crossing takes place at least 1.4 miles (2.3 km) above sea level at every point, with the first camp being at 10,000 ft (3,000 m) above sea level. The desert can be extremely hot during the day and extremely cold at night.

Welcome to one of South America's toughest races, where participants carry everything they need for seven days on their backs as they run through 30 checkpoints to the finish line. That said, water can be reloaded at the checkpoints and laptops are available for use, while weather information, shared tents for shade and rest, and medical attention are provided. Although the race starts at the highest point and gradually descends, there are still 1,683 m (5,521 ft) of ascents to deal with. Stage 5 is known as 'the Long March', with a distance roughly double that of the previous stages, and the highest elevation gain in one day, 684 m (2,244 ft). Carrying enough food to provide sufficient calorific intake can be a challenge.

The concept and level of difficulty compare with the Marathon des Sables, as well as the other desert races organised by 4 Deserts and Racing the Planet, such as the Gobi March and the Sahara Race. Daytime temperatures in the Atacama often reach 30°C and sometimes soar as high as 46°C, but because nights cool down as far as 6°C, racers need to carry more clothes, and because the campgrounds are rocky, they need to carry a camping mattress.

Among the rewards are the desert's natural wonders, including its volcanoes. The region's few inhabitants include Aymara and Atacama Indians, who live traditional lives herding llamas and alpacas. Sacred sites and ancient paintings pepper the landscape. And there are simple pleasures such as running down sand dunes.

Some people just can't get enough of desert racing, such as South Korea's Jesse Yoo, who has at least 20 under his belt, having completed the entire 4 Deserts series twice.

PROFILE

'My heart is strong,' said Vladmi dos Santos at the 2013 Atacama Crossing, explaining that he saw the race not with his eyes but his heart, and that he was very happy to have made friends with all the competitors. 'The people see me as a normal person, not blind,' he said. Dos Santos, who works with Brazil's Paralympic Committee, was guided by American firefighter Erin Leighty and won the Spirit Award. Kejiro Hamada of Japan was the second blind participant in the Atacama Crossing that year, the longest foot race either had attempted.

Also competing was Canadian Jim Willett, who had overcome colon cancer only three years earlier, and started participating in the 4 Deserts series to celebrate life and prove that anything is possible. Ian Bond, meanwhile, was racing to raise funds for the Santa Barbara Rescue Mission; the place where he had found 'the answers to maintaining a higher quality of life after nearly 30 years of addiction'.

Vladmi was back for the Atacama in 2014, this time guided by fellow racer Alex Silva de Lima. The Atacama Crossing race celebrated its ten-year anniversary in 2014, with 161 competitors from 36 countries being challenged by the variable terrain and temperatures and the high altitudes. As usual, many racers raised money for charities, and everyone pushed themselves to the limit physically and mentally.

STATISTICS

 Optimum weight of your daypack: 9 kg or less

 Approximate number of competitors: 200

 Countries represented: 40

 Fastest man: Vicente Garcia Beneito (Spain), 23 hours 46 minutes (2012)

 Fastest woman: Anne-Marie Flammersfeld (Germany), 29 hours 49 minutes (2012)

 Approximate slowest time (for those who walk the course): 70 hours

Litres of water consumed by racers, staff and volunteers: 15,000

Likely weight loss over the course of the week: 2 kg

BADWATER 135

What is it? Ultramarathon

Location: Death Valley, California

Established: 1987

Held: Annually in mid-July

Equipment: Running gear, sun protection, water

Distance: 135 miles (217 km)

Obstacles: Extreme temperatures up to 49°C (120°F) in the shade, tough ascents and descents over mountains, loneliness

There's no shortage of endurance events these days making grandiose claims for themselves. Organised by AdventureCORPS, the Badwater 135 is up there with the best of them, boasting that it is 'the most demanding and extreme foot race offered on the planet'. Unlike some others, however, the folk at Badwater may have a point.

The good news about the Badwater 135 is that it used to be a hell of a lot worse. Originally the race was meant to link the lowest and highest points in the contiguous United States. As such, it began in California's Badwater Basin, which lies at 282 ft (85.5 m) below sea level, and ended on the summit of Mount Whitney at a height of 14,505 ft (4,421 m). The distance was 146 miles (235 km) and the cumulative height gain was somewhere around 19,000 ft (5,800 m). At some stage, however, the US Forest Service began requiring permits for those people wanting to ascend Mount Whitney, whereupon the course was altered.

The bad news is that the race remains an awful grind. Beginning, as before, in the Badwater Basin in the heart of Death Valley, it now ends a mere 135 miles (217 km) away, 8,300 ft (2,530 m) above the sea, at the trailhead or 'Portals' to Mount Whitney. Along the way the route traverses a couple of mountain ranges, including the gaunt, eroded rock formations of the Panamint massif, which helps bring the cumulative height gain for the race to a formidable 13,000 ft (4,000 m). In the meantime, runners must also cross the notorious Death Valley, an eerily beautiful but deadly expanse of sun-blasted salt flats, interminable gravel fans, sand dunes and dry creek-beds interspersed by gaping canyons and overlooked by vertical cliffs soaring in places nearly 2 miles (3.2 km) above the valley floor. Moreover, the peculiar climate of the valley, in which the air is heated and rotated like in a convection oven, makes it, in the middle of summer, one of the hottest places on earth.

Further complicating matters, there is no course support. Runners must organise their own vehicle and crew who are responsible for providing everything from food and water to pacing, gear and first aid. The race has a 28-hour cut-off point at Panamint Springs resort. Those runners who manage to complete the course within 48 hours receive a belt buckle and a medal. There is no prize money involved.

PROFILE

In the summer of 2002 the Badwater Hall of Fame was inaugurated with the induction of its first member, Al Arnold, in recognition of his efforts in founding the race. That year's Badwater was run on the 25th anniversary of his epic 84-hour trek from Badwater Basin to the summit of Mount Whitney.

A superb athlete and child of California's Human Potential movement, Arnold was the first person to successfully run the Badwater course. He did it at the age of 50 on the third attempt after four years of incessant struggle and grind. His first attempt, in 1974, ended after only 18 miles (29 km) when he was struck down by dehydration. In describing the experience, which left him weak, vomiting and unable to breathe, Arnold said it was as if someone had hit him 'in the middle of the stomach with a 16-pound shot'.

Undeterred, and despite discouragement from family and friends, the following year Arnold tried again. His preparations on this occasion had been meticulous. Among other things, he had taken to riding an exercise bike in a 200°F sauna, working in 45-minute sessions in order to acclimatise himself to the heat and stress of the desert. Unfortunately, however, Arnold's preparations were in vain as this second attempt, made in a relatively cool 105°F, came to grief after 50 miles (80 km) when he damaged his right knee. In 1976 he decided not to take on the course when he broke down during a training run.

By now, Arnold admits, he had a 'Death Valley obsession'. Accordingly, when he set out from Badwater before dawn on 3 August 1977, on what would prove the hottest day of the year in the valley, he was determined to succeed no matter what. On this occasion, he says, he 'ran with humility', having taught himself to run a 20-minute mile while keeping his pulse rate to a steady 120 beats a minute. He had also come to recognise the power of the mind on such occasions and was now adept at putting himself into a trance-like state.

Running in what he called his 'Lawrence of Arabia garb' – a tennis hat with flannel shield to protect his neck and shoulders – and placing 'one foot in front of the other, going from rock to rock', Arnold finally reached his goal. Fifty metres from the Mount Whitney summit, he sat down and did some exercises, in order, he says, to get some silence from the trekkers who previously had been applauding his run. Finally he stood up and, after looking up at the sky, walked slowly and deliberately to the top of the mountain. He had no sooner reached it than he broke down in tears.

STATISTICS

Record for the initial 146-mile (235-km) course:
33 hours 54 minutes set by Marshall Ulrich (1991)

Record for amended 135-mile (217-km) course:
22 hours 51 minutes 29 seconds set by Valmir Nunes (2007)

THE WORLD'S TOUGHEST RACES

 Fastest woman: 26 hours 16 minutes 12 seconds, Jamie Donaldson (2010)

 Number of competitors annually: 90

 Percentage of dropouts: 20–40 per cent

 In the early years of the race there was no set route and runners looked for the shortest ways. In the inaugural race a runner named Adrian Crane used cross-country skis to cross the salt flats at Badwater

SPINE RACE

What is it? Non-stop winter race along the entire Pennine Way

Location: England

Established: 2012

Held: Annually in January

Equipment: GPS, camping gear (the lighter the better), running/ warm clothes, head torch, stove, ice spikes

Distance: 268 miles (431 km)

Obstacles: Snow, hail, ice, mud, wading through bogs; long distance, arduous terrain, hills

The Pennine Way, perhaps the most demanding National Trail in Britain, crosses some of England's most challenging terrain, ending at Kirk Yetholm in the Scottish Borders. From Edale in the Peak District, it passes through the Cheviots, the Yorkshire Dales and Northumberland National Park, and in winter the weather is unpredictable and often reaches Arctic extremes.

The Spine Race is, therefore, unmistakably gruelling, debatably Britain's most brutal. A combination of freezing temperatures, fierce wind and rain make hypothermia a risk; competitors tackle the slippery moonscape of Malham Cove and climb a waterfall at Cauldron Snout. Mark Caldwell, who finished the Spine in 2012 and 2014, wrote, 'The compulsory baggage doesn't get any lighter; sleep is a luxury...' Darkness and harsh conditions make camaraderie and the ability to use a GPS essential. On the other hand, the Way passes through villages with the opportunity to fuel up on chips, pasties and the like – if you get to the shop before the other racers, or to the pub before closing!

After the first 50 miles (80 km), it's a mental game. Exhaustion is a serious problem, with beds only available for limited use at checkpoints, and many racers put off camping or bivvying out for fear of losing time. The longest day is day two, with 60 miles (97 km) between checkpoints and an average completion time of 22–30 hours; a 'run-through' checkpoint halfway has medics and food. The five main 24-hour checkpoints provide one substantial serving of hot food per person, water and medical assistance, and racers are checked for hypothermia and cold-weather injuries.

PROFILE

Ian Bowles signed up for the 2012 Spine Challenger – a 108-mile race starting from the same point – but had to pull out and passed on his entry to fellow runner Mark Brooks, saying if Mark won, he could let Ian have the prize of entry to the 2013 Spine. Mark did win and so 57-year-old Ian accepted the challenge he'd jokingly set himself to do the full 268 miles (431 km) the next year. Although having no expectations about completing, he took the race seriously, being careful to control body temperature by changing layers of clothes, as being too cold or too hot wastes energy.

A couple of wrong turns lost him some time, however, so in order not to fall behind he opted not to stop at an open pub to eat. This, he admitted, was a mistake, as he was already very hungry. The missed opportunity led to nausea, and the medics at the next checkpoint, seeing his condition, insisted he lie down and take in dextrose, cola and porridge. All this on day one. He'd learned a lesson. The next day, he resolved not to pass any food stops, even making small detours to cafes and shops. His favourite snack was a large jacket potato baked at the checkpoint with half a stock cube inside; wrapped in foil, it stayed warm for six hours inside his down jacket. Late on day five he stopped at a pub hoping for food, but they'd stopped serving. He saw some abandoned plates of half-eaten food and ate the lot.

The strategy worked: Ian finished the Spine. His head got him to the end, he wrote.

STATISTICS

 Finishers in 2012: 3

 2012 record: 151 hours 2 minutes (Gary Morrison and Steve Thompson)

Fastest man: 110 hours 45 minutes set by Pavel Paloncy (2014). The Czech was unsupported, beating the previous year's record by 14 hours

THE WORLD'S TOUGHEST RACES

 Fastest woman: 153 hours 17 minutes set by Debbie Brupbacher (2014)

 Weight carried by winning teams, including water: Less than 10 kg

 Shortest distance between checkpoints: 32.95 miles (53 km) (checkpoints two and three)

 Ascent: 38,580 ft (11,759 m)

 Highest point: 2,930 ft (893 m)

 Number of competitors annually: 125

 Qualifying points for the Ultra-Trail du Mont-Blanc: 4

CHAPTER 4

STONE

OXFAM TRAILWALKER

What is it? Ultramarathon that began as a Gurkha training exercise

Location: Hong Kong

Established: 1986

Held: Annually in November

Equipment: Running gear

Distance: 62 miles (100 km)

Obstacles: Steep climbs, technical descents, steps

The Oxfam Trailwalker Hong Kong began in 1981, when Hong Kong was still a British colony. Back then it was a training exercise for the Queen's Gurkha Signals, a section of the Gurkha Brigade in the British Army. In 1986, the race underwent a change when, for the first time, civilians were allowed to compete and Oxfam Hong Kong became involved in its organisation.

In 1997 it underwent a further permutation after Hong Kong reverted to Chinese rule and the Gurkhas were relocated to Britain. While those hardy souls continued their annual rambles across Sussex's picturesque South Downs, in Hong Kong the event continued without them. At the same time the move to the UK spawned a new wave of Trailwalker events under the Oxfam aegis. Nowadays 15 individual races, spread across 11 different nations, take place annually. The Hong Kong race event remains the largest, however, with 4,800 runners competing every year.

Evoking the military virtues of teamwork and unison, competitors race in teams of four that are required to negotiate each checkpoint, and cross the finish line, together.

The course unfolds around the outskirts of the city. It is part road, part trail and views of the striking urban landscape alternate with sections of verdant tree cover. Ten stages of varying lengths make up the 62 miles (100 km), with a cumulative 14,700 ft of elevation gain testing competitors' stamina and strength. While the first section of the course, comprised of flat road and gentle hills that lead up and around the Hong Kong coast, is relatively mild, the mid-section turns ferocious, with steep climbs, technical descents and an inordinate number of stairs. The finishing section brings competitors home gently, with a descent by road followed by a stretch of dirt track that leads around a reservoir. By then, however, the cards are well and truly on the table and the tameness of the course only serves to highlight the manic drive of the competitors as the leading teams strive to achieve ultimate supremacy.

PROFILE

In 2013 another promising field lined up with two Nepalese teams, Team Nepal and Columbia S1, among the favourites. Significantly, the leaders of each of these teams, Samir Tamang and Ram Kumar Khatri, had both been members of the Salomon Bonaqua Racing team that had come second the previous year.

The race proved to be a perfect example of how the teamwork system can influence the outcome. It also saw Hong Kong politics raise its head early on when protesters, upset by a recent development, blocked the course at the first checkpoint. The race was immediately rerouted, forcing Team Nepal to do some backtracking that saw them surrender the lead to their opponents. The two Himalayan teams were soon neck and neck again, however, passing through checkpoints together and going up and down hills at a breathtaking pace.

After negotiating Tai Mo Shan, the race's toughest ascent, they remained deadlocked at Checkpoint 8 with a mere 13 miles (21 km) to run. At the 9-mile (15-km) mark, however, running with headlamps, a Team Nepal member began to cramp. This allowed the Columbia team to establish a lead and set the scene for a dramatic finish. Another spurt by Team Nepal saw the teams exchange leads and, covering each kilometre in a little over four minutes, Samir Tamang's men established a significant break over their rivals so that victory looked assured.

However, just to prove the old adage that a chain is only as strong as its weakest link, a little before the final checkpoint Team Nepal's Aite Tamang went down with cramp and the cards were back on the table. Urged on by his teammates, Tamang, who had finished 13th in that year's Ultra-Trail du Mont-Blanc, rose to his feet and staggered on. The two teams crossed the last checkpoint in unison but shortly afterwards Tamang was again stricken by cramp. The Columbia team streaked ahead as Tamang dropped out.

The two teams had pushed each other to remarkable feats. Team Columbia crossed the line in 10 hours 58 minutes, which was not only a new record but also the first time in the race's 27-year history that a team had gone under the 11-hour mark. Second running Team Nepal completed the race in 11 hours 1 minute.

STATISTICS

Winning team 2013: Team Columbia, 10 hours 58 minutes

Runners-up 2013: Team Nepal, 11 hours 1 minute

Total number of competitors since 1986: Over 81,000

Amount raised for Oxfam since 1986: Over HK$422 million

2012 was a record-breaking year with the first three teams home all completing the course in under 12 hours

DRAGON'S BACK RACE/RAS CEFN Y DDRAIG

What is it? Running on remote and trackless terrain down the spine of Wales

Location: Welsh wilderness from Conwy Castle to Carreg Cennen Castle

Established: 1992 but wasn't run again until 2012

Held: Varies

Equipment: Fell-running gear

Distance: 186 miles (300 km) in five days

Obstacles: 15,000 m of ascent

The Dragon's Back Race takes runners from north to south, up and down the slopes of the wild, ruggedly beautiful spine of Wales. They run from checkpoint to checkpoint, climbing around 51,000 ft (15,544 m), often with no marked paths – thus testing mountain craft as well as running skills. It is seen as one of the toughest mountain races on the planet and one coveted by ultra runners, especially since the legendary race has been held so few times.

The route encompasses the famous mountains of Snowdon, the Moelwyns and Rhinogs, Cadair Idris and the Black Mountains. Low cloud can make visibility a problem, as is navigation along lonely and fearsome rocky ridges. Richard Askwith, in his book *Feet in the Clouds*, said: 'If you stop concentrating on your map and compass for a moment you will be lost.' Temperatures can be hot in the day and very cold at night. Medics can treat dehydration, blisters and exhaustion at camp, where racers wash in mountain streams.

It is estimated that faster competitors will be on their feet for eight hours a day; the back of the pack may take 18 hours to reach the same target. Of the 85 who started in 2012, only 32 finished. In pre-registration for the 2015 race, only 150 of 293 applications were accepted. Race director Shane Ohly says competitors must demonstrate an ability to stay safe as well as a reasonable chance of finishing the tough course. Lots of events claim to be the toughest in the world, 'so competitors don't really believe you when you say it... but we meant it!'

A film of the 2012 edition of this legendary race won several awards in 2013 and Matt Heason of Sheffield Adventure Film Festival called it 'one of the great running documentaries'. Claire Maxted of *Trail Running* magazine, who reported on the race, said the film conveyed both the stunning mountain scenery and the 'tough-as-nails attitude of the runners' and gives an insight into 'the hardships they are willing, or not willing, to endure'.

PROFILE

It's such a demanding course, it's hardly surprising that the first ever Dragon's Back Race in 1992 was won by a woman.

Helene Diamantides, who says she is 'very competitive', had in 1987 set a new record for running from Everest Base Camp to Kathmandu with Alison Wright in 3 days and 10 hours, beating the previous Sherpa record by 12 hours. In 1988 she set a new women's record for the Bob Graham Round in the Lake District, as well as winning the Mount Cameroon Race and Mount Kinabalu Race in Borneo. In the summer of 1989, she ran all three British 'rounds' – the Bob Graham, the Paddy Buckley and Ramsay's Round – and was the first person to complete all three in one year, alongside Adrian Belton. The Fell Running Association named her Long Distance Fell Runner of the Year.

In 1992, she competed in Wales against the great ultra and mountain runners of the world, such as Rune Larsen, three-times winner of the Spartathlon, Stefan Schlett, the world's most prolific endurance runner, and three teams of Paras from the British army. There were fewer participants in races such as this, yet the standard was extremely high. But Helene is low key about her victory that day, saying fell running back then was simpler, just 'a good long day out in the hills'. She admits, though, that the kit these days is much more comfortable than stuff like the 'itchy woolly balaclavas' they used to wear.

She says what makes British fell running tough is the navigation required in bad weather conditions and on varied terrain. Dependence on GPS devices takes away some of the challenge and she suggests they could be used only in emergencies, with time penalties for their use.

Twenty years later, a mother with much less time to train, she still came fourth.

STATISTICS

1992 results (overall time for five days)

Pairs category:

 1 – Diamantides/Stone, 38 hours 38 minutes

 2 – Belton/McDermot, 39 hours 11 minutes

 3 – Walford/Clarke, 41 hours 22 minutes

Solos category:

 1 – Redmayne, 42 hours 59 minutes

 2 – Larsson, 44 hours 41 minutes

 3 – Collister, 46 hours 41 minutes

2012 results (overall time for five days)

 1 – Steve Birkinshaw, 43 hours 25 minutes 30 seconds

 2 – Rob Baker, 45 hours 22 minutes 27 seconds

 3 – Patrick Devine Wright, 49 hours 2 minutes 4 seconds

 4 – Helene Whitaker, 49 hours 10 minutes 5 seconds

BUFFALO STAMPEDE ULTRA SKYMARATHON

What is it? Out and back SkyMarathon over the Victorian Alps

Location: Victoria, Australia

Established: 2014

Held: Annually in April

Equipment: Windproof coat, 500 ml fluids

Distance: 47 miles (75.5 km)

Obstacles: Four climbs – not only Mount Buffalo but also Mystic, Clear Spot and Keatings Ridge – out and back again, adding up to 14,911 ft (4,545 m) vertical

This challenge, sadly, has nothing to do with stampeding buffalo but is named for Mount Buffalo, which provides the gruelling but impressive terrain. The idea of a SkyMarathon in a country that's mostly flat desert is unusual, but in the south-east corner of Australia between Melbourne and Sydney are the Alps of Victoria, the highest peaks. Mount Buffalo, a plateau rising to 3,300 ft (1,005 m), is a protected area, and one of Australia's oldest national parks, established in 1898.

The old-fashioned township of Bright on the Ovens River, dating from the Gold Rush days of the 1850s, now draws cyclists, mountain-climbers, kayakers, fishermen and paragliders, so it was only a matter of time before skyrunning came to the Victorian Alps. Also on offer is a 16-mile (26-km) and a 26.2-mile (42-km) race, but the Ultra SkyMarathon is a 47-mile (75.5-km) event – the first skyrace in Australia, held for the first time in April 2014, described by one racer as 'beautifully brutal'.

Competitors start out in Bright – although it's actually dark when they set out before dawn, using headlamps – to spend the day slogging up and down four peaks on fire trails and near-vertical slopes in conditions that can be muddy and slippery, with the 'Big Walk' up to Buffalo Chalet. In the inaugural race, each runner was timed from the base to the summits of Mystic (over 1,640 ft/500 m vertical), Clear Spot (over 1,640 ft/500 m vertical) and Buffalo (over 3,280 ft/1,000 m vertical). The competitor with the lowest combined time won a prize of $1,500 for being King of the Mountain – a race within the race.

PROFILE

Dakota Jones from the USA already had plenty of skyrunning experience under his belt and yet was surprised by how challenging the race turned out to be. The event was theoretically no harder than anything he'd tackled before in Europe or the USA, and the peaks looked gentler, but they weren't. Running and climbing through the Australian bush was 'much more difficult than I could have believed'.

Ben Duffus, one of a team of four from Queensland, Australia, had hopes of catching up with Dakota at one point in the race, but found himself tripping over a rock as he tired, and crawling up the mountain on his hands and knees until at last he gave up. Two of his teammates also did not finish.

The landscape had a toughness Dakota could only describe as 'primeval', and the only thing that got him through the last two climbs, he says, was experience, still doubting all the way that he would make it. The winner of the inaugural Buffalo Stampede Ultra SkyMarathon, he said, 'I didn't feel triumphant. I just felt glad to be done.'

STATISTICS

Elevation gain: 14,911 ft (4,545 m)

Elevation loss: 14,911 ft (4,545 m)

Maximum altitude: 4,527 ft (1,380 m)

Number of aid stations: 8

Cut-off time for competitors: 17.5 hours

Average time: 12 hours 34 minutes

Winner in 2014: Dakota Jones (7 hours 48 minutes 3 seconds)

Age range of winners: 18–29

STONE

 Oldest finisher: 59

 Number of competitors in 2014: 127

 Number of finishers recorded: 98

Longest time in 2014: 16 hours 58 minutes 47 seconds

RAMSAY'S ROUND

What is it? Mountain marathon – 24 Munros in 24 hours

Location: Scottish Highlands

Established: 1978

Held: Any time

Equipment: No rules

Distance: 60 miles (97 km) approx.

Obstacles: 28,500 ft (8,690 m) of climbing

On 9 July 1978, Charlie Ramsay, a member of Lochaber Athletic Club in Fort William, ran down Ben Nevis just before noon, setting a record: he had climbed 24 Lochaber Munros in 24 hours. A round of 19 Munros had been completed in 1964 by Philip Tranter, travelling anticlockwise, but Ramsay extended it to 24 in as many hours. Ramsay's record wouldn't be broken for nine years.

A Munro is a Scottish mountain over 3,000 ft (914 m) high, and Ramsay's dream had been to bring the fell-running style of the Lakeland runners of Cumbria to the Scottish Highlands. The route includes Ben Nevis, the Aonachs, the Grey Corries, the Easains, the Loch Treig Munros and the Mamores ridge.

In 1986, Chris Brasher was on a business trip to Edinburgh when he called in to Ramsay's office to find out more. Brasher had been instrumental in helping Roger Bannister achieve his first sub-4-minute mile in 1954 and was the original organiser of the London Marathon. Having worked for years towards building public interest in competitive orienteering, he had the contacts needed to make something more of Ramsay's Round. Ever since, there has been a steady flow of successful attempts of the mega-classic every year.

Today contenders for Ramsay's Round can compete in either direction, though most take the round clockwise, starting with Ben Nevis. All must start and finish at Glen Nevis Youth Hostel. Because a Ramsay's Round can be completed at any time, competitors can choose dates based on weather conditions. A full moon can be helpful for night navigation.

The other two famous rounds in the UK are the Bob Graham (42 of the highest peaks in the English Lake District in under 24 hours, first achieved by Bob Graham at the age of 42) and the Paddy Buckley (47 peaks of Snowdonia, Wales).

PROFILE

At the age of 49, Tom Phillips of Lancaster completed the 24 Munros in December 2012 in 26 hours 57 minutes, three hours faster than his previous winter best. He had finished in under 23 hours with three other runners in summer 2011, but winter is a much harder challenge with the more extreme weather and limited daylight. 'No comparison!' he said. Though some say that good snow conditions can be better than drizzle and mud; plus, there tends to be more people around in the summer.

Phillips set out at 6 p.m. and had temperatures of around −10°C until daylight. That's a lot of cold and dark. But the lack of wind was a bonus, and the main reason he had chosen to make the attempt at that time. There was snow and ice. 'I lost lots of time on some ascents where crusty snow lay on top of powder − extremely fatiguing,' he said.

The highlights for him were going up Ben Nevis in the dark, with Fort William below under a veil of cloud, and then shooting stars the following night as he ran towards his last Munro. They took his mind off his toes freezing into his shoes.

STATISTICS

 Number of successful attempts prior to 2011: 60

 Fastest men's completion time: 18 hours 23 minutes, Adrian Belton, August 1989

 Fastest women's completion time: 19 hours 38 minutes, Nicky Spinks, May 2014 (also the fastest time that year)

Fastest winter completion: 23 hours 18 minutes, 23–24 February 2014, Jon Gay*

---

* The summer completion for the same racer was 23 hours 7 minutes.

ULTRA-TRAIL DU MONT-BLANC

What is it? One-stage ultramarathon

Location: Mont Blanc massif

Established: 2003

Held: Annually in August

Equipment: Minimum equipment required for safety reasons include a waterproof jacket, warm clothes, food, water, a whistle, survival blanket and head torch

Distance: 104 miles (168 km)

Obstacles: Heavy snow, rain, treacherous wind, night sections, mountainous terrain

Circumventing the Mont-Blanc massif, the Ultra-Trail du Mont-Blanc, or UTMB as it's frequently known, is billed, somewhat grandly, as 'the race of all the superlatives'. It may well be one of the world's most scenic ultramarathons and is regarded as one of the toughest.

The route follows the Tour du Mont-Blanc hiking path, which thousands of walkers tackle every summer. Yet while these enthusiasts, delighted by alpine meadows, sparkling glaciers, carpets of wildflowers and gleaming white peaks towering above stupendous valleys, take anywhere between seven and 10 days to complete the route, competitors in the UTMB are required to do it in less than 46 hours.

The UTMB is organised by Les Trailers du Mont-Blanc, whose ideals include solidarity between runners and respect for the environment. The ultramarathon begins in Chamonix, in France, and crosses into Italy and Switzerland before finishing back in Chamonix.

Crucially, much of the race is run above 8,202 ft (2,500 m) and the overall height gain is a challenging 31,500 ft (9,600 m). Though runners are required to carry the majority of their food and water, food and drink points are scattered along the route and there are also four major 'life bases' that provide hot meals, beds and, for those so inclined, massages.

The UTMB is now regarded as the most popular ultramarathon in Europe.

PROFILE

After winning the 2012 Ultra-Trail du Mont-Blanc, when the course was shortened due to inclement weather conditions, François D'Haene went into the 2014 race a firm favourite. However, the genial Frenchman, who likes to spend time with his family and run his own winery in between races, claims that he never goes into a race expecting to win. On the contrary, he maintains that runners must be modest in their ambitions and describes himself as a novice in each race that he enters. When, as has occurred with some frequency in recent years, he happens to win a race, he regards it as 'a present'.

For three days before the 2014 UTMB D'Haene was troubled by stomach problems, which only abated once the race was under way. The man who believes that his main opponents are the mountain and the distance, rather than his fellow competitors, then proceeded to run what many believe was the perfect race.

From the start of the race to the 67-mile (108-km) mark at La Fouly, D'Haene either led or shared the lead with Spaniards Tòfol Castanyer, Iker Karrera and Luis Alberto Hernando. Subsequently, and seemingly without effort, between La Fouly and Champex-Lac he established a 10-minute gap between himself and the rest of the field in the space of only 8.5 miles (14 km). From that point on he upped his dominance, gradually increasing his lead as he homed in on a new course record. He eventually crossed the line in 20 hours 11 minutes 44 seconds, which was 22 minutes faster than the record set the previous year by Xavier Thevenard. He was nearly 45 minutes in front of Castanyer and Karrera who took second place together.

STATISTICS

↑ **Highest point on the UTMB:** Grand Col de Ferret, 8,323 ft (2,537 m)

Number of competitors when it began in 2003: 700

Number of competitors in 2004: 1,400

Number of competitors in 2014: 2,434

THE WORLD'S TOUGHEST RACES

 Number of competitors who failed to finish or were timed out in 2014: 852

 Male record: 20 hours 11 minutes 44 seconds set by François D'Haene in 2014

 Female record: 22 hours 37 minutes 27 seconds set in 2013 by American Rory Bosio, who came seventh overall. Her time slashed an astonishing 2 hours 20 minutes off the previous record. Bosio also won the 2014 women's event

MONGOLIA SUNRISE TO SUNSET

What is it? Trail run/adventure marathon

Location: Mongolia

Established: 1999

Held: Annually in August

Equipment: Rain gear, sun protection and warm clothes, water bottles, electric torch

Distance: 26.2 miles/62 miles (42 km/100 km)

Obstacles: One of the world's hilliest ultras

The 'MS2S' was ranked among the 25 Best Adventure Marathons in the World by *Men's Journal*, and *Asia Trail* magazine lists it in the top 20 'must-do' ultras in Asia. It's easy to see why – even the name sounds somehow perfect. It is a beautiful trail run which many say they will remember for the rest of their lives. And it's not only for the place, but the people.

Runners from around the world gather less to test themselves than to experience the wonders of Mongolia, raising awareness for the conservation of the alpine Lake Khövsgöl, called the 'Dark Blue Pearl of Mongolia' or 'mother lake' by locals, one of the largest single bodies of drinkable fresh water in the world. It's a feelgood race, with everyone enjoying not only the environment but the sense of contributing something worthwhile.

The marathon begins in the dark in windblown, wooded lowlands, rising 2,400 ft (732 m) to Chichee Pass, with inspiring views of Khövsgöl National Park. The classic alpine scenery of mountains, meadows, lakes and wildflowers is given a unique Mongolian twist thanks to herds of yaks and reindeer, wild horses, yurts and shaman monuments. The tracks pass through marshy forest, over steep, rocky mountain passes and around the lake.

The MS2S is organised on a non-profit basis and proceeds go towards keeping the pristine mountain area beautiful and supporting the unique local nomadic culture, thanks to the ecoLeap Foundation. The programme includes hiring park rangers and raising awareness nationwide about keeping the natural environment rubbish-free. Many participants spend extra days at Camp Toilogt horseback riding, hiking and kayaking. The event aims to contribute as much as possible to the local economy, to show that preservation of the park and the culture will support their livelihood. Locals are hired to set the course, local doctors supervise aid stations and locally produced cream, instead of imported butter, is used for meals.

Among the endorsements for the event on the website are a few very special ones from local people such as a herder who said the event added 'a page of history to Khövsgöl'.

PROFILE

The fifth MS2S in 2003 proved a special event in many ways. The day started on a magical note, with a local musician playing bird calls on a flute at 3.30 a.m., and a wolf being sighted near the camp before the racers set out at dawn. Unusually for the time of year, the first mountain pass was covered in snow and fog.

After the Chichee Pass, the UK's Clive Jones was just 30 minutes behind defending 62-mile (100-km) champ Nuuree Enkhtur of Mongolia. All other contenders were at least 30 minutes behind him. As they entered the second half of the race, Jones closed Enkhtur's lead to just 7 minutes. Behind him were Catherine Worth from the UK (who had won the 100k women's category the year before), Trevor Goh from Australia (a MS2S novice) and Mark Progin from Switzerland (a third-time competitor, who had cycled 994 miles (1,600 km) across Mongolia to get to the ultramarathon, and warmed up a few days before by running the 26.2-mile (42-km) race).

Well, Enkhtur pulled ahead, as did Goh and Progin. By the 55-mile (88-km) mark, Goh was running alongside Enkhtur, enjoying the scenery and finding that if he focused on the small figures in the distance, soon he would overtake them. Goh finished the race 20 minutes ahead of the reigning champion with a time of 12 hours 23 minutes.

And what happened to Clive Jones? Well, it's quite possible that he was conserving his energy. He was, after all, in Khövsgöl for his honeymoon.

He wrote later that 'The mother-in-law came too and I still had a fantastic time. I leave Mongolia with a Mongolian wife, some fantastic memories, and an irresistible urge to come and run again as soon as possible.' Perhaps he was the winner after all.

STATISTICS

 Elevation at race start: 5,397 ft (1,645 m)

 Accumulated elevation gain/loss for marathon route: 7,398 ft (2,255 m)

 Accumulated elevation gain/loss for ultra route: 11,040 ft (3,365 m)

 Maximum time allowed: 18 hours

 Number of runners in 2013: 80 from 22 countries

 2013 winner (62 miles/100 km): Jonas Schenk, 10 hours 44 minutes

 2013 winner (62 miles/100 km), women's: Sarah Edson, 13 hours 55 minutes

 2014 winner (62 miles/100 km): Sean Smith, 13 hours, 37 minutes

 2014 winner (62 miles/100 km): Rhonda Stricklett, 14 hours, 25 minutes

 Oldest participant in 2014: Mark Progin, 69 years old

 Qualifying points towards Ultra-Trail du Mont-Blanc: 2 (ultramarathon only)

# KAIHŌGYŌ

What is it? A 1,000-day challenge running around a mountain, on a seven-year spiritual journey to enlightenment

Location: Japan

Established: Origins in 831

Held: Completed only 46 times since 1885

Equipment: Straw sandals, white robes and hat, walking stick, rope and knife

Distance: Roughly the same distance as the circumference of the earth

Obstacles: Wild boar, various stations of worship and people wanting to be blessed along the route

If you really want to test your body to the absolute limit, and feel the need for a supreme level of spiritual enlightenment, you might want to consider joining the so-called Marathon Monks of Mount Hiei. Of course, you would have to become a monk to participate, which is somewhat extreme. Their temple was established back in the early 800s on the site where the God Fudo Myo-o appeared to a young boy called So-o. So-o turned out to be quite a monk, curing people from terminal illnesses and relieving them from demonic possessions. Among the monks that gathered at the temple it became the custom to complete a term of 100, 700 and 1,000 days of chanting and visiting stations of worship around the mountain.

During the first three years of the 1,000-day challenge, the monks who take on this challenge complete 100 consecutive daily marathons of 18.5 miles (30 km) in each year. In the years four and five they step up to 200 consecutive daily marathons each year. They then have to complete a seven-day fast without food, water or rest. In year six the marathon distance is increased to 37 miles (60 km) and they have 100 days of that. The final year the distance increases again to 52 miles (84 km) for 100 days and then one final burst of 100 days doing the original 18.5-mile (30-km) route.

Taking on the challenge comes with a fairly gruesome twist. Once a monk has completed the first 100 days of the challenge and made the decision to complete the next 900, should he then give up, or fail to complete the challenge for any reason, he is honour bound to commit suicide. Indeed, he has to carry a rope and a knife for exactly that purpose for the entire duration of each run. Although there have been no instances of this since the nineteenth century, there are unmarked graves along the way as a reminder of where monks took their lives.

PROFILE

Yusai Sakai struggled at school. Born in 1926, he failed his end-of-school exams and signed up for the Japanese war effort. At the end of the war he tried again to get into university but failed. He ended up drifting through a series of dead-end jobs. He opened a noodle restaurant in Tokyo but it burnt down. He married but his wife committed suicide when he was 40. So in 1965, he travelled to the Mount Hiei monastery and appealed to the monks to be taken into their number.

They wouldn't let him join them but they did kindly allow him to undertake a special prayer ritual that involved standing under a freezing waterfall and rising from his knees 108 times (108 being a significant number for a great many faiths including Buddhism). That strengthened his faith, and presumably his knees as well, and he was allowed to join the order.

Sakai completed the 1,000-day challenge and was given the title of Saintly Master of the Highest Practice, but he didn't stop there. 'I didn't feel satisfied, I could have done a lot of things better,' he said. And so, one year later he started it all again, and at the age of 61 Sakai became one of only three monks ever to complete the Kaihōgyō twice.

Sakai's fame spread beyond Japan. He continued to walk and made journeys into China and India, and was presented to Pope John Paul II in 1995.

STATISTICS

 Time taken by novice monks to complete the final 1,400 ft (427 m) climb back up the mountain: 45 minutes

 Time taken by monks who have completed the 1,000-day challenge to complete the final 1,400

ft (427 m) climb back up the mountain: 20 minutes

 Pairs of sandals used per day in tough conditions: 4–5

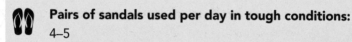 **Places of worship to be visited on each circuit of the mountain:** 270

CHAPTER 5
MULTI-
DISCIPLINE

 # BARKLEY

What is it? Foot race 'set up for you to fail'

Location: Cumberland Mountains of eastern Tennessee

Established: 1985

Held: Annually towards the end of March

Equipment: Outdoor gear for all weathers, food, water

Distance: 100 miles (161 km)

Obstacles: Barely marked course over mountainous, overgrown terrain; temperatures that can change from icy to steaming within hours; rain, snow, sleet, fog, mud, flooding; psychological tricks

You might refer to the Barkley as 'quirky' or 'amusing' if it wasn't so perfectly gut-wrenching. Certainly competitors have little to laugh about during this 60-hour assault on body and spirit, which has been called everything from 'a satanic running adventure' to 'the race that eats its young' and might just well be the most brutal endurance event on earth.

The race's director and creator, Gary 'Laz' Cantrell, who summons runners to the starting line by blowing a conch shell and plays the theme 'Taps' on a bugle for competitors who drop out, is unapologetic about the race's intentions. 'All the big races are set up for you to succeed,' he says. 'The Barkley is set up for you to fail.'

Cantrell designed the race with friend Karl Henn after reading of the escape of James Earl Ray, the assassin of Martin Luther King Jr, from Brushy Mountain State Prison in the heart of the Tennessee mountains. The fact that Ray was at large for 54 hours but was found, in extremely poor shape, only 8 miles (13 km) from the prison, made a big impression on them. In 1985 the pair went up into the mountains and devised a route, which local Park Rangers immediately declared impossible.

The course consists of five 20-mile laps around the perimeter of Frozen Head State Park. There are no aid stations, just water at two separate points. The cut-offs are 12 hours for each loop, which might sound a lot until you consider the course. Features inclined to slow you down include 'Little Hell', a 1,500-ft (457-m) climb over two-thirds of a mile with a gradient of 50 per cent, 'Son of a Bitch Ditch', which is 20 ft (6 m) wide and 20 ft deep, and 'Checkmate Hill' which ascends 1,300 ft (396 m) over a quarter of a mile. Thorny saw briars calculated to tear your legs to shreds adorn the colourfully named 'Testicle Spectacle'. There's also 'Big Hell', another formidable ascent, as well as a quarter-mile tunnel that runs underneath the now defunct prison's exercise yard, which is pitch dark and half-full of water.

Adding to the fun (as well as ensuring that competitors complete the loops), along the way runners must find hidden books from which they are required to tear the page corresponding to their race number. Titles like *A Time to Die*, *Southern Discomfort* and *What to Do When You Feel Lost, Alone, and Helpless* contribute to the macabre spirit of proceedings.

PROFILE

A race that begins not with the crack of a pistol but with the lighting of a cigarette, and in which the prize for those who finish (there are no actual 'winners' in the Barkley) is that they get to stop running, is bound to be singular. The fun begins when potential competitors attempt to enter the race.

The Barkley doesn't have anything as conventional as a website. Nor is it ever announced when, exactly, the race will take place or how runners go about entering. A web of lies and deceit, designed to confound and intimidate newcomers, as well as an aura of Masonic-like secrecy surrounds the entire process. As Cantrell, whose goal is to make things as mentally stressful for runners as possible, somewhat cryptically explains, 'people who have business out there on the Barkley find out how to enter.'

At the same time, every year there's at least one competitor whose lack of aptitude for the event would suggest that he definitely doesn't have business out on the Barkley. Cantrell, who openly mocks competitors, claims that he includes these 'virgins' to provide amusement for himself and the other runners.

The entry fee for the race is a modest $1.60. However, in yet another bizarre twist, first-time participants must also bring a number plate from their home state, while seasoned runners have been asked to provide everything from flannelette shirts to cartons of Camel cigarettes. Everyone who wishes to run, moreover, must send Cantrell an essay arguing why they should be allowed to do so and answer whimsical and seemingly meaningless questions like: What is the most important vegetable group? If that's not confounding enough, entries must also be lodged on a specific day. Competitors who fail to do so risk being disqualified.

STATISTICS

    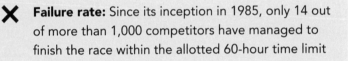

Failure rate: Since its inception in 1985, only 14 out of more than 1,000 competitors have managed to finish the race within the allotted 60-hour time limit

Distance: Initially only 55 miles (89 km); it was four years before anyone managed to complete it. The distance was lengthened to 100 miles (161 km) and another six years passed before anybody finished

Overall height gain: 60,000 ft (18,288 m) (equivalent of climbing Everest twice from sea level)

Number of competitors: No more than 35, due to restrictions enforced by Tennessee Park

Course record: 55 hours 42 minutes 27 seconds, Flyin' Brian Robertson, 2008 (the course was immediately altered for the following year's race)

Cantrell named the race after a friend of his, Barry Barkley, who was injured in Vietnam and so is unable to run. Barkley is a farmer who's busy planting each year when the race is held. Apparently he's seen it once.

MEN'S HEALTH SURVIVAL OF THE FITTEST

What is it? An urban obstacle race

Location: London, Nottingham, Manchester, Edinburgh, Cardiff

Established: 2008

Held: September to November

Equipment: Robust trainers and kit that dries quickly

Distance: 6.2 miles (10 km) (at least)

Obstacles: 200 of them including hay bales, ice baths, builders' skips full of water, traffic barriers, tyres, monkey bars, abandoned cars, sandbags, fire hoses, sports stadium steps

In 2003 Jim Mee was trekking in the mountains of Peru when the idea of creating urban adventure competitions came to him. He staged his first event in 2004 with 300 competitors kayaking, climbing and abseiling around the city of Edinburgh, which was televised on Channel 4. Since then he has gone on to build a business called Rat Race, which organises a series of endurance challenges including the *Men's Health* Survival of the Fittest.

The competition is staged in successive UK cities over a period of five weeks in the autumn every year. Waves of competitors set off in intervals for a 6.2-mile (10-km) run interspersed with a selection of obstacles. The course will vary from city to city but you can expect things like rope nets over ice to crawl under and heavy sandbags to be carried over traffic barriers. Some of the challenges might require a little assistance from your fellow competitors to negotiate but pretty much everyone finds a way to get round most of the obstacles.

With its motto of 'Blood, Sweat and Beers', there is a large emphasis on the after-party and Jim Mee does his best to organise a decent beer tent and some post-race entertainment. After all, these city types that are attracted to his events love to party.

PROFILE

Freelance writer Vicky Lane took part in the London competition in 2014 when the race had moved from Battersea Power Station to Wembley. As a keen runner Vicky was conscious that a lack of upper-body strength might leave her struggling to haul herself up and over the obstacles. However, with a friendly shove from a fellow competitor at the first set of hay bales, and with the support of a group of friends, she soon started to enjoy herself, particularly as one of her teammates turned into a human bowling ball when slipping on a muddy slope.

Although all the members of her team had difficult moments around the course, including one of them having a little cry on top of one of the walls, the quartet pulled together, forming a human pyramid to get themselves over the highest obstacles. In the end Kate finished in 2 hours 13 minutes 56 seconds, placing 5,121st out of 5,908 competitors, with her friends finishing alongside her. As Kate said, 'This isn't just fun. It's really fun.'

STATISTICS

Participants in 2008: 1,000

Participants in 2014: 30,000

Results for London Survival of the Fittest 2014

Total number of competitors: 5,908

Fastest times

Male: 48 minutes 18 seconds, Jonathon Albon

Female: 1 hour 4 minutes 15 seconds, Lucy Marlew

Average time

Male: 1 hour 42 minutes 15 seconds

Female: 1 hour 49 minutes 41 seconds

DEATH RACE

What is it? A 48+ hour race where the challenges are kept secret from the participants

Location: Pittsburgh, Pennsylvania, USA

Established: 2005

Held: Annually in summer and winter

Equipment: Varies – in 2013 participants were told to bring a bag of pennies, 10 lb (4.5 kg) of onions and a book on the Greek language

Distance: 40 miles (64 km) (or 60 miles (97 km) if you go off course)

Obstacles: Barbed wire, nettles and thorns, freezing lakes, bizarre cooking and farming tasks

While working as a Wall Street trader, Joe De Sena took part in Ironman challenges in his spare time. In 2005 he met another athlete, teacher and swimming coach Andy Weinberg. The two of them found themselves discussing how racers can become 'soft' because they know what to expect and can train for the challenges. The two of them created a race where none of the participants would have any idea what to expect. The race attracts around 300 elite athletes who put themselves and their fate entirely into the hands of the race organisers.

The participants are then subjected to a variety of physical and mental challenges, such as diving to retrieve their bag of pennies, learning obscure quotes, running, crawling and scrambling over between 40–60 miles (64–97 km) of difficult terrain. There are cruel tricks throughout. In 2009, participants carried a bicycle for 10 hours only to ride it for five minutes. The organisers have designed the race with the express intention of finding the breaking point of the participants.

In 2014 only 10 per cent of the participants finished. As they say on their website, 'Awards will be presented to those that finish. We don't plan on handing out too much.'

PROFILE

Experienced mountain climber Mark Jenkins took part in the Death Race in 2010, aged 51. In the build-up to the race he increased his standard daily workout (100 sit ups, 100 push ups, 100 pull ups and 30 minutes running up and down a sports stadium staircase) to include running on ski slopes with a backpack.

Along with the other 89 participants, Mark's Death Race included running with a wheelbarrow of manure, carrying a 7-ft wooden footbridge in teams of eight, crawling along a 200-yard barbed-wire trench, splitting logs, translating Greek text, chopping and eating raw onions, and an assortment of lung-busting hikes, runs and ice-cold pond swims. In the end he quit after 21 hours.

Only 19 people finished the race, with the last straggler coming in after 39 hours. The race had turned out to be 45 miles (72 km) long with an ascent and descent of 22,000 ft. Mark spent the next two days in a wheelchair, packing his aching knees with ice, and took a further six weeks of physiotherapy to recover.

Stephanie Bishop, on the other hand, who was the first woman to finish the 2010 race and the sixth finisher overall, said afterwards, 'I loved that race. It was like three Ironmans back to back. I had sooo much fun.'

STATISTICS

The following details were released after the 2014 race:

 Time taken: Between 42 and 47 hours

 Distance covered: Between 60–90 miles (87–145 km) (60 if you stayed on course the whole time, extra mileage for wandering)

 Total weight of wood gathered: 550+ lb (250+ kg)

 Height of tree climb every racer had to complete: Approx. 30 ft (9 m)

 Total number of raw eggs consumed: 72

Example of quote learnt and recited during the event:
'Of all the wonders that I yet have heard,
It seems to me most strange that men should fear,
Seeing that death, a necessary end,
Will come when it will come...'

William Shakespeare (*Julius Caesar*)

PATAGONIA EXPEDITION RACE

What is it? 'The Last Wild Race'

Location: Chilean Patagonia

Established: 2004

Held: Annually in February

Equipment: Long list of mandatory equipment includes everything from head torch to gaiters, flare, compasses, kayak, mountain bike and climbing rope

Distance: Approx. 435 miles (700 km)

Obstacles: Savage terrain, intense weather

Quite apart from the naturally spectacular, untamed environment where this challenge takes place, in a region where so many dream of going, several things set the Patagonia Expedition Race apart.

First, there's an element of exploration. 'Some of the areas we go into, we may be the first people to have gone there,' says Pete Clayden, who moved to Chile in 2011 and helps organise the race. The expedition element involves a search for new places including previously unknown mountain passages, with the 2016 route pushing deep into untouched, rugged territory in Chile's extreme south. The race director, Chilean geologist

Stjepan Pavicic, plans a route that takes in mountains, fjords, glaciers and iceberg-filled lakes. To a certain extent, teams choose and navigate their own route to the finish, making strategy and teamwork as important as endurance. Endurance certainly counts, though, in a race that takes over a week and often results in sleep-deprived hallucinations.

Secondly, it is a multi-discipline event that can require trekking, mountain biking, kayaking and climbing, and unlike many events, you cannot register for the Patagonia Expedition Race unless you can prove ability. You must be able to swim and have experience of sea kayaking, orienteering (at least one team member must be able to use a compass and triangulation techniques) and handling ropes (e.g. abseiling and rappel, river crossing) in order to pass the pre-race practical evaluations. At least one team member must have a first-aid certificate.

Finally, it's very much about teamwork, with each team of four requiring at least one man and one woman. Entrants come from nations around the world but the Brits have been leading the pack in recent years, with Mark Humphrey having been on the winning team for four years. France and New Zealand follow closely behind in the number of first-place wins. After ten years, the race took a break in 2014–15 but is back up and running for 2016. There again, 2013 had been a particularly challenging race.

PROFILE

The US team GearJunkie Yogaslackers – Jason, Chelsey, Daniel and Paul – went into the 2013 race hoping for a first place, having come fifth, second and third before.

They were also hoping for the adventures, sweat and tears and 'delirious laughs' that they'd experienced in previous years. Being gear junkies, of course, they had added a piece of equipment – a live tracking device, so followers of the race could see where they were and exchange messages with the team. They had been training intensely for months and felt strong.

The Yogaslackers are interesting because the team includes a husband and wife – who apparently are still married after doing this for years. Generally spouses avoid being on the same team together, but maybe the fact that they are both yoga instructors in Oregon allows for a certain inner calm.

Just hours before the race, Paul became violently ill, losing 'every calorie and ounce of free water from his body', as teammate Daniel put it. It cost them dearly on the overnight bike ride to the glacier on day one, but they still finished the stage in fourth place. Fierce winds from the very outset were making a tough course even tougher, with speeds of over 100 mph knocking riders off their bikes. Four teams retired after failing to meet the time limits on the 15.5-mile (25-km) trek across Glacier Tyndall with its maze of crevasses.

After leaving the glacier, the team had a critical conflict. It was almost night, and bitterly cold. The other members overruled the captain's suggestion that they go ahead with the crossing, but they lost time by taking a different route. Looking back, Daniel believes, they could have saved hours by waiting for morning and crossing the lake at first light. Two days in, only six teams out of

11 were still active. The teams were far enough apart that the Yogaslackers already felt there was no chance of improving their placement. Then Daniel got sick with diarrhoea, and Chelsey suffered a fungal infection on her foot, a twisted ankle and tendonitis in her shin. She was only able to proceed with painkillers.

With an unexpected snowstorm at checkpoint 15, the race was a challenge from start to finish for all involved, even the seasoned veterans. Out of 11 teams at the outset, only three teams finished. Even the chirpy Yogaslackers said they finished 'stronger as friends, but knowing that a lot would have to change before we could do it again'. Limits had certainly been tested, but everyone left transformed, having seen places that few ever will.

STATISTICS

2013 finishers

Fastest time: Team Adidas Terrex Prunesco (UK), 9 days 6 hours 55 minutes

Second place: Team Eastwind (Japan), 10 days 20 hours 50 minutes

Third place: Team GearJunkie Yogaslackers (USA), 10 days 21 hours 5 minutes

THE WORLD'S TOUGHEST RACES

 Average sleep per night: 1–2 hours

£ Prize money: 0

2012 hero: Japanese woman Kaori Waki, who broke a rib on day two but continued, helping her team to achieve third place

TOUGH GUY

What is it? Perhaps the toughest cross-country assault course in the world

Location: Perton, near Wolverhampton, England

Established: 1987

Held: Biannually in January/February and July

Equipment: Thin layers of lightweight, fast-drying clothing e.g. thin-skin Neoprene, not cotton; hat and gloves, anklets to protect against rope burns, mud cream for Nettle Warrior (to prevent the nasty combo of sunburn and nettle stings)

Distance: 9 miles (15 km)

Obstacles: Fire, tunnels, freezing water and about 200 more…

Tough Guy started as an 'old-fashioned cross-country run', with man-made obstacles added. The idea was to create between one and ten more obstacles for every event. Today, after more than a quarter of a century of Tough Guy, there are roughly 250 obstacles and it claims to be the 'toughest test of its kind anywhere in the world'. Participants sprint across burning bales of hay and crawl through pipes and thick mud under barbed wire. They abseil down 130-ft (40-m) ropes and cross fields laced with electric cables while wet. The Tough Guy course is designed to test your fear of heights, tight spaces and much more. It is seen as 'the world's safest, most dangerous one-day survival ordeal'.

Don't imagine that the summer Tough Guy event is any easier. Oh no. Held in July, it's called 'Nettle Warrior' and includes all of the original obstacles but adds chest-high stinging nettles.

In 2005 there were 23 fractured bones. Founder Billy Wilson says, 'If people break their legs, they don't come back whining like many in our blame and claim culture.' They apologise and ask if they can come back next year.

The events are supposed to be fun, however: Jelly Babies are handed out along the course, and at the end you get a blanket, hot chocolate, tea and biscuits. Numbers are restricted to 7,000 for both Tough Guy and Nettle Warrior. And, unbelievably, tickets sell out and in some years they have had to turn a thousand people away. The sense of achievement seems to be worth all the pain. Entry fee rises month by month to encourage early enlisting. It's now a fully international event and there are no gender/upper age barriers: anyone can pit themselves against the course with a 'family of equals in front, behind and around'. The lower age limit is 18 and 16–17 year olds may participate if accompanied by a parent or guardian, though the phrase 'scarred for life' comes to mind.

PROFILE

Wilson was once famous for taking part in the first London Marathon dressed as a pantomime horse. He loves a bit of publicity, and is not afraid of controversy. He drew criticism from church leaders in 2000 for his 'Tough Guy Jesus' event, when contestants set out on the course carrying wooden crosses weighing 30–40 kg for the first 1,000 yards (914 m) of the race, in commemoration of

Christ's walk to the crucifixion, to mark the millennium. 'Jesus was the original tough guy,' he explained. But 'He taught us to love each other.' That year, Aled Rees from Cardiff, five-time winner, finished at the front of the pack again with a time of 1 hour 46 minutes.

Wilson is affectionately known as 'Mr Mouse', but is a former Grenadier Guardsman and the obstacles are often military-inspired: there are Gallipoli Snipers, Great War Trenches, a Battle of the Somme Mud Ditch Crossing, a Vietcong Torture Chamber, Stalag Escape, the Killing Fields... You get the picture. Rumour has it that shotgun blanks are fired throughout the course, and military participants have claimed the course is tougher than the army. Wilson has said, 'We are trying to re-create the First World War and Vietnam battlefields to show people what their granddads went through.'

The Germans have been winning the race for the past few years. Knut Hoehler won three years running, 2011–13, and 21-year-old Charles Franzke in 2014. He had previously competed in Getting Tough – The Race in Germany and said in an interview that more and more people in Germany were getting into obstacle-course racing. He trains hard: 'I often walk in cold rivers and do some push-ups in the water.'

STATISTICS

 Fastest time in February 2014: 1 hour 29 minutes (Charles Franzke)

 Time ahead of second place: 1 minute (Paul Jones)

 Fastest woman in February 2014: Friederike Feil, 1 hour 54 minutes

 Time ahead of second-place woman (Katrin-Stefanie Nussbaum): 13 minutes

 Number of nationalities competing in 2014: 30

 Oldest competitor: Patrick Barnes first came to Tough Guy at the age of 84

 **Lake temperature:** –2 to –10°C

 Number of cups of hot chocolate served at each event: Approx. 10,000

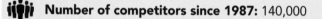 **Number of competitors since 1987:** 140,000

 Number of entrants in February 2014: 3,503

 Number of actual competitors in February 2014: 3,003

Number of finishers in February 2014: 2,228

MULTI-DISCIPLINE

 Number required for male or mixed team to compete in team trophy contests: 8

 For all-female teams: Minimum 5

 Average number of shoes lost on course per event: 740

Shorter course: 6–7.5 miles (10–12 km) with 180 obstacles

SPEIGHT'S COAST TO COAST ('THE LONGEST DAY')

What is it? A multi-sport endurance event

Location: South Island, New Zealand

Established: 1983

Held: Annually in February

Equipment: Mandatory equipment includes a fully equipped bicycle with lights and repair kit, bike helmet, timing transponder, running shoes, a first aid kit, reflective ankle bands, a suitable and appropriately equipped kayak

Distance: 150 miles (243 km)

Obstacles: Challenging ascent on foot into the Southern Alps, including river crossings, rapids on kayak descent of the Waimakariri River

At first glance a brewery might seem an odd sponsor for a world-class multi-sport endurance event. However, there's no questioning the credentials of the Speight's Coast to Coast 'Longest Day', which is regarded internationally as one of the greatest and longest-running adventure races in the world.

In 1982 sportsman Robin Judkins and 11 friends got together to pioneer the course that forms today's Coast to Coast. The first official race was held the following year when a grand total of 79 competitors attempted what would prove a seminal multi-sport adventure event. The race was originally designed to be completed over two days, but in 1987, aiming to up the ante and retain the Coast to Coast's reputation as an elite sporting event, Judkins introduced a one-day version that he named, appropriately, 'The Longest Day'. Today this remains the highlight event of the competition, although there is also a two-day single competitor event and a two-day tandem event. Categories for men and women apply.

Attracting premier athletes from across the globe, the Coast to Coast begins on the black sands of Kumara Beach on the west coast of New Zealand's South Island. After a 1.8-mile (3-km) run competitors climb aboard bikes for a 34-mile (55-km) ascent along the banks of the Taramakau River to the foothills of the Southern Alps. The cycle leg is followed by another run, this time a gruelling off-trail slog up the Deception River valley, with several river crossings through icy mountain water thrown in for good measure. Thirty kilometres from where they started, and 800 m higher, competitors negotiate 'Goat Pass' and begin their descent towards the east coast. The running leg ends at 'Klondyke Corner', where competitors in the two-day event stop for the night.

Competitors depart Klondyke Corner on bikes for a 9-mile (15-km) cycle to the shores of the Waimakariri River. Upon arrival they jump aboard kayaks for what many consider the highlight of the race, a 43-mile (70-km) paddle along a winding water course which, descending from the heart of the Alps into the Canterbury Plains, negotiates a stunning gorge and rapids that may reach Grade 2 in size. The race concludes with a 43-mile (70-km) cycle that brings competitors to New Brighton Pier on the Pacific Ocean.

In 2013 Robin Judkins sold the Coast to Coast to the Queenstown-based Trojan Holdings Limited after 31 years at the helm.

PROFILE

New Zealand athlete Richard Ussher began his international career as a skier, representing his country in the freestyle skiing event at the 1998 winter Olympics in Nagano, Japan. After retiring from skiing he felt the need for another challenge. The catalyst for his move into the discipline of multi-sport adventure racing came from seeing the Coast to Coast on television. That particular race was won by the legendary Steve Gurney and, says Ussher, it looked like 'a bit of fun'.

Ussher subsequently competed in the 2000 Coast to Coast, in which he placed a respectable seventh. It was a solid start to a sterling career that has seen Ussher win five Coast to Coast races, hold the NZ Ironman triathlon record, been proclaimed the Adventure Racing World Champion twice and won the Abu Dhabi Adventure Challenge on four separate occasions. As a professional athlete, Ussher motivates himself by setting goals and challenges but the main thing that keeps him going, he admits, is his love of the sport.

In 2008 Ussher relinquished adventure racing in order to pursue Ironman triathlete events. He subsequently returned to multi-sport after deciding that his primary passion was for off-road racing and also discovering that it was hard to keep going without the prize money that adventure racing provides. Ussher admits that he is often compelled to compete in events that provide the chance of winning prize money at the expense of events he would ideally prefer to take part in. One of the attractions of retirement, he claims, is the opportunity to compete only in races that he really wants to do.

In training Ussher focuses on the disciplines in which he wants to excel. Although he devises his own training schedules, he also relies on trusted outsiders to observe proceedings and ensure that, as he says, 'I'm not getting too carried away.' Time is occasionally a problem and he admits to having experienced various 'meltdowns' that have required him to have a break from sport. His most trusted adviser is his Finnish-born wife and fellow multi-sport racer, Elina, with whom he often teams up for adventure events.

STATISTICS

£ **Prize money for men and women's one-day event:** First prize is NZ$10,000 (approx. £5,000), prize for second place is NZ$2,000 (approx. £2,000) and the prize for third is NZ$1,000 (approx. £500)

 Men's one-day record: 10 hours 34 minutes 37 seconds set by Keith Murray (1994)

 Men's two-day record: 11 hours 5 minutes 18 seconds set by Keith Murray (1993)

THE WORLD'S TOUGHEST RACES

 Women's one-day record: 12 hours 9 minutes 26 seconds set by Andrea Murray (1997)*

 Record number of wins: 9 by Steve Gurney (1990, 1991, 1997, 1998, 1999, 2000, 2001, 2002, 2003)

*Andrea, a US citizen, was married to Keith Murray; both were living in NZ at the time.

THE RACE

What is it? Self-supported endurance running, kayaking and cycling race

Location: North-west Donegal, Ireland

Established: 2014

Held: Annually in early March

Equipment: Compulsory equipment includes bike with lights, repair kit and helmet, luminous clothing, waterproof clothing, whistle, mobile phone, water bottles or hydration pack

Distance: 155 miles (250 km)

Obstacles: Poor weather conditions including possible rain, hail, sleet, snow, fog and gale-force winds, and a race that just doesn't seem to stop

North-west Donegal isn't the warmest place in early March – made even worse if you are one of the 100 competitors who have chosen to subject themselves to the tortures of The Race. According to the event's creators, Sand2Snow Adventures and Gartan Outdoor Education Centre, The Race is designed to provide competitors with one of the toughest and most memorable events of their lives. To this end the wintry season has been expressly chosen to maximise the chances of encountering horrible weather.

The Race begins before dawn at the Gartan Adventure Centre on the shores of Gartan Lake. In a thick darkness that's bound to be cold and may also be wet and windy or even, possibly, snowing, competitors set off on a brisk half-marathon. The 13.5-mile (22-km) run ends on the banks of Lough Swilly where competitors leap into kayaks for a 9-mile (15-km) paddle.

Upon regaining dry land up towards the north-west tip of Ireland, competitors leave their kayaks behind in favour of bicycles for a ride up hill and down dale along a section of wildly spectacular coast. After 96 grinding kilometres, the riders arrive at the base of Muckish Mountain. Abandoning their bikes they must set off on foot up the mountain and then run, crawl or scramble back down again. Over a distance of 3 miles (5 km) competitors gain and then lose a torturous 1,640 ft (500 m).

Back on their bikes, the now physically challenged competitors head off on a final dash around the appropriately named Bloody Foreland. Seventy kilometres later, they relinquish their bikes for the last time and engage on a final full marathon, which takes place, in total darkness, amidst the natural splendours of Glenveagh National Park. Some time before dawn and the 6 a.m. finish time, the first competitors arrive back at the Gartan Adventure centre on the shores of Lake Gartan, having completed 155 miles (250 km) within 24 hours.

The Race is limited each year to 100 competitors in order both to minimise impact upon the environment and enhance the quality of the experience. It is a non-profit event, the proceeds of which go to Self Help Africa to help rural Africans achieve economic independence.

PROFILE

According to organisers, there is no standard type of competitor in The Race. On the contrary, the event draws a diverse range of people hailing from all manner of backgrounds and disciplines.

In 2015 Swiss athlete Patrick Utz competed in his second Race. Utz's goal is refreshingly simple: he aimed to catch up with old friends, better his time and 'be a good man again on March 7'. This alone provided him with the motivation to train hard or, as he says, 'to kick my arse into shape'.

Utz is a late starter to extreme activity. Until late 2007, he maintains, he was 'a couch potato' and a poor example to his children. Now he sees the chance to compete in events like The Race as both a privilege and an opportunity to fulfil another dream. A firm believer in the ideal that 'if you dream it, you can do it', Utz declares that in his job as a sales coach he sees two types of people: those who dream on a large scale and those who, in his words, 'are prisoners of their own dark castle'. The dreamers are by far the more fortunate.

The Race appealed to Utz on a number of levels. He enjoys more challenging events, he says, because there are fewer starters. Normal Ironman events he finds overcrowded and also far too commercial. Utz is also inspired by the opportunity to be close to nature and to find himself challenged by it.

In preparation, Utz employs a coach who monitors his work and ensures that he doesn't overdo things. To keep from burning out or peaking too early, his training is undertaken at roughly 65 per cent of his capacity. Most of his work is aerobic and includes running, swimming, cycling and sessions on a treadmill with a bit of weight training thrown in. He trains six days a week, in sessions ranging from one hour to anything up to five hours on Saturdays. Sundays are rest days which he spends with his family.

In general, his diet during training is aimed at simulating race conditions. Thus he refrains from loading up on carbohydrates in order to get his body accustomed to burning fats and proteins for energy. The idea is to make his body more efficient on the principle that during a race athletes are unable to consume as many calories as their bodies want to consume.

STATISTICS

 Number of competitors in 2014: 54, from nine countries

 Number of finishers within the allotted 24 hours: 35

 First place in 2014: Bill Wells (Canada), 15 hours 22 minutes

 Entry fee: €600, which includes two nights' accommodation, various meals, use of equipment, access to trainers and discounts for family and friends in local restaurants

SPARTAN RACE

What is it? Down and dirty multi-terrain obstacle course

Location: Worldwide

Established: 2010

Held: Throughout the year

Equipment: None required

Distance: 3/6/12.5 miles (5/10/20 km)

Obstacles: Tarzan swings, sandbag carries, mud runs – it's always changing

Founded by eight people obsessed with extreme sports including a marathon runner, a mountaineer and a marine, Spartan Race ran their first event in Vermont, USA, in 2010, aiming to make it the toughest race on earth – quite a feat. Moreover, they wanted to encourage people to get off their couches and into the outdoors to have fun while overcoming obstacles and achieving a new self-confidence.

They are setting up new Spartan Races around the world every year, with 2014 seeing 80 Reebok Spartan Races take place in North America, Europe and Australia. The first Spartan Race in Asia took place in South Korea in November 2013. Each course is unique so competitors will never race the same course twice, and course maps are not available before the race. Primarily it's a trail race featuring mud, water and obstacles such as crawling under barbed wire or jumping over fire, and signs and helpers guide participants through the course.

There are three levels: Sprint, Super and Beast; complete three in a calendar year and you earn your Spartan Trifecta. All races are timed, judged and ranked but Spartan Race is an inclusive experience, open to all including beginners and focusing on transformation: 'a way to become more than you were yesterday' – fitter, more connected and more courageous. In other words, Spartan is about bringing endurance racing to the masses. It's also a great team or charity event. Everyone receives a finishing medal.

PROFILE

Andrew Picazo had been overweight all his life but decided a month after his daughter Yolanda was born in February 2013 that he wanted to become healthier for her: at the time he weighed 375 lb (170 kg). He and his friend Walter would take the challenge together. They started off changing their diet, but then hired a personal trainer, Master Jo'el Ramirez, who took them through all types of workouts and talked to them about his experiences with Spartan races. 'I was in awe, but in my head I thought I can never do that.' Then one day, Ramirez said they were going to do the Spartan Sprint.

So he started rigorous training. He hiked up steep hills for miles three or four times a week. He watched videos of Spartan Races to help him adopt the mindset. They intimidated him as he'd never done anything like that before; but he was also impressed by 'the amount of love the online Spartan community shared'. Their help and encouragement helped him get past his doubts.

By the time race day arrived, he weighed less than 229 lb (104 kg). The trainer joined Andrew and Walter for the race. 'Never in a million years would I have thought that I could run up a hill with buckets of rocks, nor jump over a seven- or eight-foot-high wall!' The Spartan Race had been one of the best experiences of his life, physically and mentally.

STATISTICS

 Number of competitors in the first Spartan in Vermont: 500

 Number of competitors today: 1 million participants in 10 nations

 Sprint: 5+ km, 15+ obstacles, 95–99 per cent finish rate

 Super: 10+ km, 21+ obstacles

 Beast: 20+ km, 26+ obstacles

 Junior age range: 5–13 years

Number of burpees you have to do if you can't pass an obstacle: 30

XPD

What is it? Expedition-length team adventure race

Location: Australia – location changes every year

Established: 2004

Held: Every 18 months

Equipment: Adventure Racing World Series mandatory list (including survival and first aid kit), plus whatever else you think you'll need

Distance: 435 miles (700 km)

Obstacles: Navigating on unmarked trails, cycling in the dark, keeping up the calorie intake

Australia being a vast country with such a wealth of remote regions, the folks at XPD decided to make full use of the range of terrain from tropics to ocean to outback, and hold each event in a different location. In the years from 2004 to 2014, the XPD went to: Broken Hill, Tasmania; Whitsunday Coast; Australian Alps; Cairns; Tasmania West Coast; and Flinders Ranges. Entries sell out within hours of opening; the XPD is a stage of the AR World Series, qualifying winners to enter the world championship.

Australian Triathlete magazine, covering the first XPD, called it 'as much an expedition as a race'. Teams of four trek, kayak and mountain bike for five to ten days, day and night, with a few other activities such as caving and abseiling thrown in for good measure. All team members must complete all sections and never be separated by more than 100 m, making it a real co-operative race where you rely on your teammates. Teams are unsupported but may send plastic trunks of equipment to forward points on the course. The onus is on the team to decide what equipment, food and drink they will need – particularly tricky when the exact route is only made available 24 hours before the start. Spectators can follow the progress of the teams on the live website, as they wear satellite tracking devices.

With epic adventures every day in remote regions, it can be hard to find enough calories to keep up energy levels when you're burning 10,000–15,000 a day. On the first XPD, the winning team only slept for one hour in three days. Unexpected windstorms affected their ability to keep on course during the kayak sections. Once they knew they had a comfortable lead, they were able to enjoy the last stages and the amazing outback landscapes. By the end, all the racers enthused about the unexpected challenges and remote terrain, which made it feel like a 'real expedition'. Allowing ten days to finish made it seem an achievable goal even for the less experienced participants.

PROFILE

In the 2013 XPD in Flinders Ranges, team Rubicon came in 23rd, after 173 hours 7 minutes. In case you're wondering, that's towards the back of the pack. But one team member, David Barlow, wrote afterwards that 'the monster that was Lake Frome would become a defining moment in our lives'.

Lake Frome, contrary to its innocuous name, is a salt pan 62 miles (100 km) long and 25 miles (40 km) wide, mostly below sea level and starkly lacking in vegetation. There are no visual reference points except for the path of the sun. The only 'point of sanity', wrote Barlow, 'was a compass bearing that pointed to nothing'.

To do something like this, said Barlow, is irrational compared with our everyday lives. It is akin to the adventurers of centuries past who would have set off with maps marked 'here be dragons'. It is only those who have been there and experienced the mixture of fear, elation and exhaustion who can understand.

On the dry salt lake their mission was to find a checkpoint on an island. The sky blended into the horizon, and the lake seemed to stretch to the end of the world. For four hours, or 12.5 miles (20 km), 'Whichever way I look, it is white.' They had no way of knowing if they were walking in the right direction. They were already hallucinating from sleep deprivation. In the heat of the sun, they contended with wind and flies and listened to the crunch of sharp salt crystals underfoot. It seemed they were walking on the spot.

Then they came to water. Was this right? They held their nerve and waded for 3 miles (5 km) – until darkness fell. The struggle was now an inner one.

Finally, after 14 hours on the lake, a beacon was spotted. Barlow later said, 'Encapsulated in one leg of one race was a lifetime of experience.'

Winning seemed somehow irrelevant at that point.

STATISTICS

7th XPD, Flinders Ranges Outback South Australia, September 2013

 Distance: Approx. 466 miles (750 km)

 Winning team: Team Mountain Designs

 Winning time: 5 days 2 hours 8 minutes

 Disciplines: Trek, mountain bike, ocean kayak, roping, navigation

 Number of teams starting: 30

Number of teams finishing: 25

ADVENTURE RACE WORLD CHAMPIONSHIP

What is it? Pinnacle of adventure racing

Location: Details change every year

Established: 2001

Held: Varies from year to year

Equipment: Mandatory equipment listed in full on website

Distance: Varies

Obstacles: Varies

The Adventure Race World Series is a tournament involving qualifier events around the globe. The top two teams at each qualifier race are entered into the championship. Adventure Race is an organisation promoting sports in the natural environment with challenge, speed and stamina at the core.

To give a sample of the variety of venues, races on the 2015 calendar were:

- The GODZone on New Zealand's South Island, February–March

- Terra Viva in northern Patagonia, April

- Raid Gallaecia in Spain, May

- Expedition Africa in Swaziland, June

- Expedition Alaska, June–July

- Cameco Cowboy Tough, Wyoming USA, July

- XPD Expedition Race, Australia, August

- Raid in France, September

- World Championship in Brazil, November

Although each destination offers something a little different, the concept of adventure racing is common to all: multi-stage endurance events including a combination of disciplines such as running/trekking, mountain biking and kayaking, canoeing or rowing. Expedition Alaska involves glacier travel, ocean kayaking and coasteering, while Expedition Africa includes mountain biking 155 miles (250 km) and canyoneering. Entrants compete in teams and navigate from control point to control point, deciding for themselves when and if to stop and rest.

PROFILE

The 2014 host was Ecuador for a 430-mile (692-km), 10-stage race, and one particular participant drew a lot of attention.

Sweden's Peak Performance team captained by Mikael Lindnord had acquitted themselves well during the days of hiking, cycling, mountain climbing and kayaking. The high altitude was a challenge, as were the extreme hot and cold temperatures. They also made some navigation mistakes.

So they would have made a fairly unremarkable finish in 12th place after 146 gruelling hours, if it wasn't for the fact that their four-strong team had acquired a new member along the way: a stray dog they named Arthur.

When they paused for a food break on the eighth stage to prepare for a 25-mile (40-km) jungle trek, they saw the scruffy looking dog and Lindnord threw him a meatball. Later, as they continued through mud and forest, they realised he was following them. They had no choice but to keep feeding him, and at one point had to pull him out of the mud. At the final stage, a 37-mile (60-km) coastal kayak, Arthur the dog jumped into the water and swam with them, so they were forced to take turns carrying him.

'He was kind of in the way during the whole paddle and we had to find different paddling techniques...' Lindnord said. He jumped into the water occasionally and got so cold they had to give him their jackets. When they closed in on land, he swam to shore and they thought they'd seen the last of him, but he joined them again.

After the race, Arthur slept with the team at their hotel. They took him to a vet and applied to take him home with them to Stockholm, to be adopted by the team captain. Peak Performance started the Arthur Foundation to raise money to protect stray dogs, and Lindnord said, 'I came to Ecuador to win the World Championship. Instead, I got a new friend.'

STATISTICS

 World rankings are released on an ongoing cycle of 4–6 months

Rankings at time of publication listed the top five teams as follows:

1 Columbia Vidaraid (ESP): 624 points

2 Seagate (NZL): 550 points

3 Adidas Terrex (GBR): 508 points

4 Tecnu (USA): 498 points

5 France Green Caffte Costa Rica (FRA): 473 points

CHAPTER 6

EXTREME
WHEELS

YAK ATTACK

What is it? Highest mountain-bike race on Earth

Location: Nepalese Himalayas

Established: 2007

Held: Annually in November

Equipment: Mountain bike, helmet, sleeping bag, GPS

Distance: 248 miles (400 km)

Obstacles: Altitude climbs to 17,800 ft (5,416 m) above sea level; sand, mud and snow

From small beginnings with just a handful of competitors, today the original Yak Attack is internationally recognised as the highest mountain bike race on the planet and seen by some as in the top ten toughest bike races. Yak Attack is an eight-stage race with 39,000 ft (12,000 m) of overall altitude gain. Temperatures range from 30°C as the race travels through the hot and dusty Himalayan foothills, to –15°C at the snow-covered Thorong La pass (17,800 ft/5,416 m) a few days later. The landscapes take some beating.

Registration takes place in Kathmandu. The hefty entry fee includes two nights' accommodation after the race at a resort-style hotel in Pokhara, and flights and bike transfer back to Kathmandu, on-site masseur and bike mechanic as well as the usual support. Medical facilities are limited due to the remoteness of the course. To give a flavour of the race, one stage involves close to 62 miles (100 km) of riding, 8,850 ft (2,700 m) of ascent, in hot and dusty conditions, while another has snow and deep mud, as the air gets thinner and the temperature starts to drop. The penultimate stage starts in the dark with freezing temperatures as riders pedal to the highest point then descend in deep snow. Valley winds make the final stretch exciting, and although there's the lure of hot springs at the end, this stage sees more crashes than any other.

The Yak Attack World Challenge Series now includes two more arduous mountain bike races: Rumble in the Jungle, located on the island of Sri Lanka and first held in November 2014, and Alpac Attack in the wilds of Patagonia, one of the most sparsely populated places on earth, first held in April 2015. The concept ticks all the boxes that set adrenaline racing: inaccessible and hostile terrain and climate, and a challenge to push competitors to the limit physically and emotionally.

PROFILE

The success of Yak Attack has allowed the team to contribute to the Nepalese MTB community, financing them to compete overseas. In an effort to raise the profile of the sport and the potential benefits for young people in Nepal, one of the world's poorest countries, Yak Attack took the current male and female Nepali Yak Attack champions to Sri Lanka for Rumble in the Jungle in November 2014 and offered free entry to the 2015 Nepal race to five local riders.

Ajay Pandi Chhetri from Kathmandu, a Yak Attack Champion, is one recipient of their support, which funded a season of racing in the UK for him. Growing up in Nepal with a terrain ideal for mountain biking gave Chhetri, who is 5 ft 4 in, weighs just 106 lb and has a tattoo on his leg of a mountain-bike racer, a love of the sport. He started riding as a child on the mountain trails and won his first race at the age of 15 on a borrowed bike.

Having trained as a bike mechanic, his expertise at fixing bikes brought him into contact with foreign cyclists who encouraged him to enter his first race. He says his achievements are about hard work and preparation. 'I was always good at sports, but cycling appealed to me because it is all about an individual's effort.' He became Nepal's national MTB champion in 2009. Having won the Yak Attack four times, in July 2011 he entered his first race in the UK, the Torq Roughride on the Shropshire-Powys border, coming third out of 600 riders. The following month he took on the TransWales MTB Marathon, Britain's longest multi-day mountain-bike race at 350 miles (563 km), winning three stages out of seven and coming an overall second.

In June 2014, he represented Nepal in South Africa at the UCI Marathon World Championships in Pietermaritzburg – a dream come true for the Nepalese team, given it was their first world championship. For some of them, it was their first trip abroad.

Training in Nepal's extreme heat, cold and monsoons would stand them in good stead for any competition.

In September 2014, Chhetri became the first foreigner to win Bhutan's high-altitude Tour of the Dragon race, 166 miles (268 km) in just one day, beating the previous record by more than half an hour. The Yak Attack would certainly have been good preparation for that.

STATISTICS

 Fastest time for Stage 2: 4 hours 34 minutes

 Slowest time for Stage 2: 9 hours 30 minutes

 Ajay Pandit Chhetri's placement in the first Rumble in the Jungle: 4th

 Number of rides completed by Ajay Pandit Chhetri by 2015: Over 600

Yak Attack supports an animal welfare association, the Himalayan Mutt Foundation, which works towards vaccinating and neutering dogs in the Annapurna region.

# CAPE EPIC

What is it? A mountain-bike race for teams of two

Location: The Western Cape, South Africa

Established: 2004

Held: Annually in March or April

Equipment: Mountain bike, multi-tool, spare parts, matching kit, camping gear

Distance: 435 miles (700 km)

Obstacles: Rocks, rocks and more rocks

Kevin Vermaak left his native South Africa after graduating from university and headed for London, England, for a career in IT. After eight years he found himself looking for a new challenge and with a group of friends entered a three-day mountain-bike race in Costa Rica. Although he enjoyed the race, he had the sneaking suspicion that he could organise something bigger and better in his home country. A few months later he had resigned from his job and was on a flight home, heading for Cape Town and the spectacular scenery of Table Mountain and the Western Cape.

Vermaak attracted over 80 VIPs, sports journalists and guests to Cape Epic's launch party, and when entries opened, the 550 places were sold out in just three days with over 20 different countries represented. Today the race is open to just over 1,200 riders with competitors coming from up to 50 different countries.

As the route, which changes every year (the 2015 race began at CPUT Wellington Campus and finished at Meerendal Wine Estate), takes riders though some remote and treacherous terrain in the Western Cape over eight stages, competing in teams of two is an essential safety feature and gives the race a special character and ethos. Both riders have to complete the race and stay within two minutes of each other throughout or face time penalties and possible disqualification. How well teammates get on and support each other during the competition becomes just as important as all the expensive kit and physical training.

The world's elite mountain-bike riders compete for substantial prize money and lucrative sponsorship deals for a race that is broadcast around the world. But it is also open to amateur riders, who win their places in a lottery. They race the same course and sleep overnight between each stage in the same tented village as the pro-racers.

After just ten years, Vermaak had built a team of over 20 permanent staff working full time on the race that has now built a reputation as mountain biking's version of the Tour de France.

PROFILE

Irish former professional road-racing cyclist Stephen Roche took part in the 2013 Cape Epic with teammate Sven Thiele. As someone with Tour de France, Giro d'Italia and World Championship titles under his belt from the 1980s, Stephen was reasonably confident that he knew how to handle a bike. The Cape Epic taught him that he still had a bit to learn about what happens to bicycles when you ride them over mountains.

To start with there is a lot more that can go wrong technically, from broken cleats to overheated breaks. Fortunately for Stephen his bike was whisked away by mechanics every night and fine-tuned to perfection. He found that mountain biking involved a lot more effort in his upper body. Writing for *Bike Magic*, Stephen said, 'It wasn't my legs that were smashed. It was my arms, wrists and my hands!'

The biggest difference for Stephen was the lack of peloton riding. On the single-track paths it was virtually non-existent. He did manage to gather up a bunch of fellow riders to share the burden of riding into a strong headwind on one of the wider roads, and taught the mountain bikers a thing or two from the road-racing side of the sport.

After 49 hours 12 minutes 22.5 seconds, 434 miles (698 km) and 51,345 ft (15,650 m) of climbing, the pair crossed the finishing line at the Lourensford Wine Estate in 308th place (and 19th in their category). They then set off to continue their education and learn a little bit more about South African wine.

STATISTICS

 Average number of years of mountain-biking experience for competitors: 8

 Average age: Men 39, women 36

 Average weight: Men 172 lb (78 kg), women 130 lb (59 kg)

Total climbing:

⬆ **2014:**   48,720 ft (14,850 m)

⬆ **2013:**   52,330 ft (15,950 m)

⬆ **2012:**   53,480 ft (16,300 m)

⬆ **2011:**   47,735 ft (14,550 m)

RACE ACROSS AMERICA

What is it? A non-stop cycle race from one side of America to the other

Location: USA

Established: 1982

Held: Annually in June

Equipment: Road bike, support crew, layers of Lycra and lots of calories

Distance: 3,000 miles (4,828 km)

Obstacles: Mountains, deserts, vast open plains, more mountains, hills and sleep deprivation

John Marino was a high school and college star athlete playing American football and baseball. A weightlifting injury left him unable to compete at his original sports and so, somewhat frustrated in 1976, he was idly flicking through the *Guinness Book of World Records* looking for a new challenge. He landed on the US coast to coast cycling record and decided to give it a go. After two years of intense cycling fanaticism he broke the world record in 1978.

Marino realised that this sort of cycling challenge was so much more than just an individual test of endurance. There were the logistics, food, equipment, weather, support crew, safety and so much more involved. He felt that it had the makings of a great sporting contest and he set about creating it. In 1982 John staged the first Great American Bike Race competing against three other riders to get from Santa Monica to New York. Although Marino finished fourth and all the riders finished in widely different times, the story captivated TV audiences on ABC. The following year the competition was renamed Race Across America and from there it has gone from strength to strength.

The route has varied through the years but it is always from West to East, passing through a dozen states as it covers a distance almost one third longer (and sometimes more as it varies year on year) than the Tour de France. While the terrain varies from mountain to desert, it's essentially a road race. The fastest solo riders can cover the distance in eight gruelling, sleep-deprived days and others have to complete it within 12 days in order to qualify as official finishers. Relay teams of two, four or eight riders tend to finish a little quicker as the riders get a little more of an opportunity to sleep and recover along the way.

The contest attracts over 300 racers every year, most competing in relay teams. Less than 200 people have successfully completed the solo challenge, a tenth of the number who have reached the summit of Everest. Those who make it across the continent will have seen America at its most spectacular and beautiful and, of course, all the way from sea to shining sea.

PROFILE

Pippa Middleton, sister of the Duchess of Cambridge, brought a touch of celebrity glamour to the 2014 race. She joined her brother James and six others in an eight-person relay team. Pippa's fame and royal connections will have helped the team in their efforts to raise money for two charities: the British Heart Foundation, which had appointed Pippa as an ambassador, and the Michael Matthews Foundation which was set up to commemorate a young man who died while attempting to climb Mount Everest and helps fund an education for children who otherwise wouldn't receive one.

Pippa and her team completed the course in just 6 days 10 hours 54 minutes, taking it in turns to drive the support vehicles and averaging just three hours of sleep each night. Pippa found the night cycling fairly intimidating as they had to swerve around snakes, skunks and even deer along the route.

Pippa's bike, a custom-built Dassi 6.2 Aero Road Bike, worth in the region of £2,500, was put up for auction on eBay after the race to raise even more money for the British Heart Foundation.

Her top tip for success? Get a particularly comfy saddle.

STATISTICS

Lowest elevation: 170 ft (52 m) below sea level

Highest elevation: 10,000 ft (3,000 m) above sea level

Total climb: 100,000 ft (30,480 m)

 Fastest solo man: Christopher Strasser 7 days 15 hours 56 minutes (2012)

 Fastest solo woman: Seana Hogan 9 days 4 hours 2 minutes (1995)

CENT COLS CHALLENGES

What is it? Series of ultimate road-cycling challenges high in the mountains

Location: France, Spain and Italy

Established: 2008

Held: From spring to autumn; some routes available on alternate years

Equipment: Road/hybrid bike

Distance: Average 125 miles (200 km) per day

Obstacles: 100 cols in 10 days; climb of 14,760–16,400 ft (4,500–5,000 m) on each stage

How would you feel about climbing for two hours non-stop – and then doing it another eight times? Each day of this multi-stage cycling challenge requires close to 3 miles (5 km) of climbing. Cent Cols Challenges take place in spectacular mountain locations, including some classic climbs and some lesser-known ones, and the number of routes to choose from increases year by year, all chosen for their sensational scenery: the Southern Alps, the Cevennes, Cantábrico, the Pyrenees, Corsica and the Dolomites. The basic concept remains the same, inspired by the Club des Cent Cols: road cycling 100 cols in 10 days – a col being a saddle between two mountains or a pass from one side of a mountain range to the other.

EXTREME WHEELS

Each challenge is limited to 30 riders. Although it is not a race, riders need to finish each day early enough to recover for the next. You can skip a col on the route, as long as you make 100 in total. Resilience and training are essential and the beauty of the mountains helps you deal with the pain. All you have to do is keep cycling up one mountain pass after another.

The CCC season opens in Corsica, seen as the 'easiest' of the group because the average daily climb is under 13,125 ft (4,000 m); it is still a brute with incessantly twisting roads, but rewards riders with sea views, the scent of the maquis, cool spring water, local sheep's cheese and possible encounters with roaming pigs. CCC Dolomites started in 2012 and was established as the hardest route that year. Starting at San Pellegrino Terme near Milan with a 16-mile (26-km) climb, it takes in the infamous Monte Zoncolan, some wild, barren scenery, lakes, hairpin bends, woodland scenery, rocky skylines and views of the Swiss Alps.

Creator of the Cent Cols Challenges Phil Deeker says he had no idea that cycling existed as a sport when he was growing up. It was not until he turned 40 that he got serious about cycling. He started off by buying a bike to commute to work, and rode his first Century Challenge a year later. After riding three Étapes du Tour, he realised he needed something bigger. As he was about to turn 50, he persuaded his wife to help him take a strange holiday, and with Claire in the support car he spent July 2007 cycling nearly 2,485 miles (4,000 km), climbing 269,000 ft (82,000 m) and riding over 312 cols in the Alps, Pyrenees, Ardèche, Cevennes and Massif Central. In the early days of the journey, he cried from exhaustion and sometimes despair, but he felt a sense of magic too. 'What had happened to me when I faced up to my scariest doubts, alone in the mountains, was life-transforming.' From this, of course, he conceived the idea of the CCC.

PROFILE

Chris Pugh wrote an entertaining blog about his experience as a 'laggard' on the September 2011 Pyrenees CCC with 18 other cyclists. After nine months of training, he wrote on the very first day, 'It's apparent within five minutes of arriving that I'm way out of my league.'

Thankfully, he wasn't alone. There was Kelvin, who confessed to Phil, the organiser, after day one that he didn't think he would survive (Phil rides the whole course and watches those who are struggling and may need support). There was also Colin. At the start of the first day, they came across an unforeseen obstacle: a trail of smashed grapes from the grape-picking harvest. Colin slipped on it while handling a roundabout, going down on his face and wrist and suffering mild concussion, cracking the handlebars of his bike. He didn't make his first col.

Chris made it through the first day after 12 hours, reflecting that each day was going to be bigger than a Tour de France day, 'and we've got 10 of them back to back'. Over the coming days the heat would go up to 40°C with no shade, then drop to near freezing with torrential rain, the combination leading to a risk of hypothermia. The 'laggards group' would get bigger. Jenny ended up in the 'sag wagon' after failing to eat enough; Colin got back on the bike but the wrist injury forced him to admit defeat; Kelvin was told to stop one afternoon because of a knee injury.

On the last day, Chris took his time starting out, letting the other laggards go ahead – but then in a spurt of energy he cruised past Kelvin and Scott, and then he actually passed one of the faster groups. It was only a moment, but a happy one. It didn't matter that he wasn't King of the Mountain. Thanks to Phil's style of organisation, the CCC group of 19 rode all together to the finish line, those at the back enjoying the slipstream of the big guys at the front. Kelvin and Jenny were still there. And the whole group stopped at Chris's 100th col.

STATISTICS

 Number of riders who made the 100 cols in the Pyrenees 2011: 15 out of 19

 Number of years Mike Simpson, King of the Mountain 2011, had been training: 25

 Hardest CCC stage at time of writing: Cantábrico Stage 5 extreme version: 132 miles (212 km), 23,550 ft (7,180 m)

 Highest number of cols on a single stage in Dolomites: 15 (Stage 7)

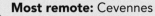 **Most technical challenge:** Pyrenees

 Best breakfast: Stage 9 of Southern Alps

 Most remote: Cevennes

TRANSPYR

What is it? Coast to coast mountain-bike race

Location: Pyrenees, Spain

Established: 2010

Held: Annually June–July

Equipment: Mountain bike, GPS, water bottle or hydration pack

Distance: 485 miles (780 km)

Obstacles: Steep mountain terrain, changeable weather with blistering temperatures interspersed with rain and cold, tough trails in places requiring technical expertise

---

Often referred to as a coast to coast mountain-bike epic, the Transpyr is more an adventure than a competitive event. It is one of those rare and happy races in which the physical intensity is matched by the prodigious beauty and cultural interest of the landscape against which it unfolds. The race begins in the Spanish seaside resort of Roses on the Mediterranean coast, and ends nearly 500 miles (800 km) away in the picturesque town of Hondarribia on the shores of the Atlantic. In riding 'coast to coast', riders traverse the high mountain passes and deep green valleys of the spectacular and historically compelling Pyrenees mountains.

Jaw-dropping scenery, ancient towns and villages, and welcoming locals with unfamiliar customs are just some of the attractions of the Transpyr, which passes through the regions of Catalonia, Aragon, Navarre and Euskadi, the Spanish Basque country.

Side by side with the adventure is the challenge of a race run over seven days and broken up into seven sections. In order to participate, riders are required to cover over 62 miles (100 km) each day and climb, on average, 8,530 ft (2,600 m) per stage. The course utilises a variety of surfaces with major roads avoided where possible in favour of local roads, forestry tracks, cross-country trails and the occasional pathless meadow where riders must dismount and either push or carry their cycles past the disinterested gaze of grazing cattle. The route is punctuated with technical sections of varying difficulty designed to test riders' proficiency.

In order to maintain the aesthetic appeal of the landscape, marking is restricted to places posing potential dangers or obscurity. Instead riders are required to use GPS on which the relevant tracks are loaded in advance. Aid stations providing food and drink are located along the route and at the end of each stage, while a meal of pasta is supplied at the end of each day. In the interests of safety and also to comply with the event's guiding principles of teamwork and solidarity, riders cannot enter individually but must form teams of two or three to be maintained throughout the race.

PROFILE

In the 2012 Transpyr, which took place over eight stages and ended at San Sebastián, temperatures when riders set out from the Mediterranean coast hovered around

45°C. However, the general consensus among riders is that stage 6, which then ran from Jaca to Isaba, provided some of the most memorable moments weather wise.

Riders were woken before dawn that morning by crashing thunder and vivid lightning. Torrential rain bucketed down, delaying the start of the race by an hour. The rain had eased by the time competitors set out, but its effect continued to be felt, most notably on an early ascent on a dirt track which had become a quagmire. Soon wheels and bike bodies became covered in a dense layer of mud, which increased their weight by as much as 10 kg.

Riders responded in various ways to the challenge. Some, the very brave (or foolhardy), persisted in trying to push or even ride their bikes, a course which entailed stopping every now and again to clean the mud from their machines. The majority, however, taking a more pragmatic view, gave their bikes a quick clean before hoisting them on to their backs and hoofing it to the end of the section.

It illustrates how competitors in the Transpyr can be both challenged and inspired as conditions place their ingenuity and resolve under the spotlight. Nor was it the end of their tribulations, which plumbed new depths when another downpour struck during an extended descent on a rugged fire track. This particular section of the Transpyr was known for its technical difficulty and certainly riders had their hands full as, with visibility reduced to a couple of metres, they bumped and skidded and slid down a stony, rutted road bisected by minor rivers. By this stage many were questioning what exactly they were doing there.

Yet, in typical Transpyr fashion, the mood altered towards the end of the day when the weather cleared and the route led them gently upwards into the embrace of a dramatic canyon. Walls of craggy granite soared upwards, while below the road a swollen river ran. The day ended well, too, with the kind of slippery slide of a trail that any rider worth their salt would die for; a fitting challenge for entry into the mountain town of Isaba with its picturesque stone buildings and network of cobbled lanes.

STATISTICS

 Cumulative height elevation over the 485 miles (780 km): 59,000 ft (18,000 m)

 Registration fee for 2015: €845

 The Transpyr organisers help individual racers find a teammate if necessary

 Competitors who wish to ride alone or are not interested in completing the whole race can take on EAST or WEST – the four stages at each end of the route

LA RUTA DE LOS CONQUISTADORES

What is it? Arguably the toughest mountain-bike race on the planet

Location: Costa Rica

Established: 1993

Held: Annually in November

Equipment: A very good fat-tyre bike and a medium racer bag of equipment – GPS, energy bars, sunblock, raingear and hydration pack

Distance: Approx. 300 miles (483 km)

Obstacles: Jungles, volcanoes, beaches – terrain generally considered unsuitable for bikes – and temperatures up to 37°C

Costa Rica's premier mountain-bike challenge is one of the toughest athletic events on earth. La Ruta traverses the American land mass from Pacific to Atlantic, crossing five mountain ranges and climbing a cumulative 29,000 ft (8,840 m) – all in just three days. Costa Rica is known as the Switzerland of Central America because of its mountain ranges.

Chris Case, managing editor of *VeloNews* who completed the course in 2013, called it 'soul-sappingly hard', taking you across 'laughably steep inclines' and 'hysterically steeper descents'. Hundreds of the best cyclists and endurance racers from around the world come to test themselves with this challenge of distance and geography, following the route taken by the Spanish conquistadors begun in the 1560s (they took 20 years to do it).

La Ruta was first cycled by Costa Rican athlete and adventurer Roman Urbina, who was captivated by the story of the Conquistadors' journey. Already known for staging challenges to raise awareness about his country's endangered wildlife, in 1993 he completed the route with 17 others and was inspired to turn it into an annual event.

Chris Carmichael, after finishing La Ruta three times, said it was possibly the hardest of all mountain-bike events on the 'epic endurance bucket list': 'It's like doing the Leadville 100 three days in a row. There's more climbing than Leadville in Stage 2 alone.' La Ruta has been going for close to a quarter of a century and is therefore considered the 'grandfather' of the multi-day mountain-bike races – loved, feared and respected.

Riders of La Ruta travel on tracks and dirt trails through nine of Costa Rica's 12 microclimates. They are drenched in the sweltering rainforest, and feel the extreme cold of the majestic 12,000-ft (3,657-m) volcanoes, riding through mud, sand and volcanic ash and over roaring rivers.

In case it's not clear, the website warns: this race 'is a test of everything you've got'. It's not so much a race as a 'personal growth journey'. The race's founder, Roman Urbina, believes that tough physical challenges are the path to a self-knowledge and understanding that can lead anyone to greatness.

PROFILE

American Brett Wolfe completed La Ruta in under 30 hours in both 2001 and 2003. Although he was not among the first to finish, he was riding, as he put it, at 'sort of a disadvantage' and wasn't expecting to be at the front of the pack.

When he was 21, in 1990, he lost most of his right leg in a motorcycle accident. He had to give up his former love of alpine skiing, and began mountain biking just a couple of years after his above-the-knee amputation. He has taken on the TransAlp challenge and TransRockies as well as La Ruta.

Some consider him the toughest MTB racer in the world. Although around half of the hundreds who attempt La Ruta drop out before the end, Wolfe, who rides without any prosthesis, has finished every race that he has entered.

For the Costa Rican challenge, where the climbing on the second day is especially hard, he says the important things are to maintain a consistent pace and manage the pain. His aim is to keep pushing himself. 'My intent is not to have people focus on me, but on what I'm doing, what is possible.'

As the organisers of the race say, La Ruta is about 'taking what you are given and coming out on top'.

STATISTICS

 Record: Federico Ramirez (Costa Rica), five-time winner

 First non-Costa Rican to finish in first place: Thomas Frischknecht (Switzerland), 2005

Top times in 2013:

 Women: Pua Mata, 14 hours 48 minutes 53 seconds

 Men: Marconi Duran, 12 hours 19 minutes 4 seconds

CHAPTER 7
WEIRDEST

? WORLD COAL-CARRYING CHAMPIONSHIPS

What is it? Coal-carrying foot race

Location: Gawthorpe, West Yorkshire, UK

Established: 1963

Held: Annually on Easter Monday

Equipment: Comfortable shoes and clothes

Distance: 3,320 ft (1,012 m)

Obstacles: 110-lb (50-kg) bag of coal, a small hill that must be negotiated

There's a refreshing lack of pretentiousness about the World Championship Coal-Carrying Race. Making no grandiose claims for itself, the event dispenses with details like entry fees, qualifications and sponsorship deals. Rather, all it demands of those brave or crazy enough to take up the challenge is that they turn up on the morning of race day at the starting point, which just happens to be outside a pub.

The Royal Oak in Owl Lane, Ossett, has been witness to the start of more than 50 World Championship Coal-Carrying Races. The majority of competitors seem to be coal-mining, rugby playing types. It certainly helps to possess a sturdy physique as men undertake the race with a 110-lb (50-kg) bag of coal slung across their shoulders.

There are two men's races and a veterans' race for competitors over 40. There is also a race for women, who are required to carry a 44-lb (20-kg) bag, and a race for children who must carry 22 lb (10 kg) and run 500 ft (150 m).

Helpfully, at the start of the race, the bags are loaded straight from the back of a truck on to competitors' shoulders. The general consensus is that, once under way, you don't want to drop your bag as you will experience great difficulty trying to pick it up again.

Bags in place, slung high up across the shoulders and gripped at two corners, the race quickly begins. Competitors are required to run 1,012 m, from the pub door to the maypole green in Gawthorpe village. The general idea is to refrain from starting out too quickly and thus conserve energy for the dreaded 'hill', which appears just after the halfway point and is more of a gentle incline but, reports suggest, tends to feel like a mountain with 50 kg on your back. Upon completing the race, competitors must drop their sacks on the green at the base of the traditional and usually freshly painted maypole.

PROFILE

Interestingly enough, the World Coal-Carrying Championships were born out of a disagreement that occurred, as disagreements tend to do, in a pub.

It was a day like any other in 1963. Enjoying a pint at the bar of Gawthorpe's 100-year-old Beehive Inn were two men, Reggie Sedgewick and Amos Clapham. The latter was a local coal merchant and would later become president of the Gawthorpe Maypole Committee. The unwitting catalyst behind the business, however, was a certain Lewis Hartley, who, entering the pub in a jovial mood, slapped Sedgewick on the back and opined that he was looking somewhat the worse for wear.

Sedgewick, unsurprisingly, took exception to the remark. 'I'm fitter than thee,' he is said to have replied, and then offered to prove it by challenging Hartley to a race. His idea, which was natural enough given the region's coal-mining history, was that they should each heave a bag of coal on to their backs and then race 'to t' top o' t' wood.'

Some say that Amos Clapham also threw his hat into the ring, claiming to be fitter than the pair of them. In any event, the conversation was overheard by a bystander named Fred Hirst, the secretary of the Maypole Committee. Hirst immediately saw a glimmer of opportunity in what the three men were proposing. More than just a contest of egos, he realised that an event of that sort could fill the local entertainment void that currently existed on the Easter Monday public holiday.

'If we're gonna 'ave a race let's 'ave it then,' he is reputed to have said. 'Let's 'ave a coil [coal in Yorkshire dialect] race from Barracks t' Maypole.' The Barracks was the name locals gave to the Royal Oak public house, which has been the starting point of the race ever since.

STATISTICS

🏆 Dave Jones of Meltham, West Yorkshire, is the undisputed legend of the coal-carrying world. Six-time winner of the World Championships, he currently holds the course record with the phenomenal time of 4 minutes 6 seconds set in 1991 and repeated, for good measure, in 1995. He holds six of the top ten times for the race

The only racer to get anywhere near Jones' record is Gawthorpe local Chris Mackie who completed the course in 4 minutes 19 seconds

Janine Burns of Dewsbury has won the women's race a staggering 11 times in succession

🏆 The current women's world record holder is three-time winner Catherine Fenton of Heckmondwike with 4 minutes 23 seconds

£ A cash prize of £750 is awarded to the winner of the men's race. The women's race winner receives £500

? KINETIC GRAND CHAMPIONSHIP

What is it? Triathlon of the art world

Location: California's northern coast from Arcata to Ferndale

Established: 1969

Held: Annually on Memorial Day weekend

Equipment: Kinetic sculpture

Distance: 42 miles (68 km)

Obstacles: Racing over sand, mud and water in a human-powered art sculpture

Over three days, the participants of the Kinetic Grand Championship race over rough terrain wearing a large piece of sculpture. Each racing team engineers a work of art from bikes and, basically, junk, creating something eye-catching that as well as having moving parts such as blinking eyes and opening mouths, can race in water, mud and deep sand. Pilots pedal and steer contraptions that in the past have resembled a giant red ant, a silver slipper, a flying saucer, a chilli pepper, a metallic chicken, a picnic basket, a 'Hippy-Potamus' with wiggling ears, vehicles covered with skulls and bones... while pit crews assist by adapting the vehicle for the different elements. *A National Geographic* blog called it 'Tour de France meets Burning Man'.

The event began in 1969 when Hobart Brown, a local sculptor, challenged artist Jack Mays to a race down the main drag of Ferndale (Brown lost). Today, the 42-mile (68-km) challenge starts on the Plaza at Arcata, California, and heads straight for the Manila dunes, where racers take on miles of sand as they make their way to the legendary Deadman's Drop. After staying overnight in Eureka, contestants prepare for a wet start to day two in chilly Humboldt Bay, where they will race through water, hoping their sculpture floats, then tackle the mile-long incline and decline of Hookton Hill before camping for the night. The final day takes them through deep mud, from the Eel River estuary through Morgan slough and back on to dry land to finish at the historic Main Street of Ferndale. Many contraptions don't make it to the finish.

Teams give out 'bribes' to judges and the thousands of spectators, many of whom follow the race teams on their own bikes. At heart, this is a bike culture event with Californian twists of art, sustainability and kookiness, and a mission for adults to have fun 'so children desire to grow older'. There are awards for art, engineering, best bribe, biggest splash, first to break down, lifetime achievement, most improved, racers' favourite volunteer... the list goes on and on, although the awards are also made out of junk. Kinetic Kops in tiny shorts may write you a ticket for wearing too much glitter or eating beef jerky while standing.

PROFILE

Reed Lacy of Corvallis, Oregon, has participated in over a dozen kinetic races over the past 20 years with his family, starting off in his home city before moving farther afield. 'We just kind of got bit by the bug,' he said. Back in 1999 he even gave a lecture on how to build cheap vehicles for kinetic races. They compete only biannually.

In 2010, he told the *Corvallis Gazette-Times*: 'My hope is to finally, some year, land on a design that actually works.' It's possible that Lacy takes the KGC a little more seriously than others. A software engineer at Hewlett-Packard, he first took part in one of these races on a co-worker's team and he took to the design element. 'He's always tinkering with stuff,' said his daughter Emily. The children didn't hesitate to tell the *Gazette-Times* how twice the wheels had come off on the sand dune leg, or how once they tipped over in the river and the sheriff had to come and get them. In spite of paddling successfully across the river section in 2010, they were unable to finish the mud bog because of a broken chain, and only won in two categories, Best Song ('Secret Racing Clan', sung to the tune of 'Secret Agent Man') and Best Pageantry. 'I didn't think we were gonna break down, but that's what you always think,' said Lacy. 'You think it's gonna work.'

In May 2012, he entered the Kinetic Grand again with 'Under the Rainbow', based on a tandem bicycle with flotation devices on the side, built to stay in low gear to tackle the sand and mud, with two large back wheels that lower to the ground for stability. He was, at last, first to cross the finish line.

'To come in ahead of everyone is quite glorious,' said Lacy.

STATISTICS
Other kinetic sculpture races in the US:

 Baltimore, Maryland; Corvallis, Oregon – 'Da Vinci Days'; Greater Port Townsend, Washington; Boulder, Colorado; Klamath, Oregon (2015 theme: Chariots on Fire)

 Number of entrants at the Klamath Kinetic Challenge 2014: 8 (one powered by Reed Lacy and his youngest daughter Ellie)

🌍 **Places where kinetic sculpture races started but didn't catch on:** Perth, Australia; Warsaw, Poland

Rules of Kinetic Grand Challenge:

- 'In the event of sunshine, the race shall proceed'

- Competing contraptions must carry a teddy bear for the purpose of comforting losing racers

- Arrows, anchors and grappling hooks prohibited

- All racers must bring a toothbrush

- Children aged 12 and over are allowed to ride the sculptures as 'barnacles' and can be replaced during the water sections by a non-human weight equivalent

- ACE awards are given to racers who finish 'without being caught either cheating or pushing their vehicle'

- If another racer honks their horn at you, you mustn't hog the road but must move to the right and allow them to pass

? WORLD BOG SNORKELLING CHAMPIONSHIPS

What is it? Snorkelling two lengths of a water-filled trench in a peat bog

Location: Llanwrtyd Wells, Powys, Wales

Established: 1985

Held: Annually on August bank holiday

Equipment: Snorkel, flippers; wetsuits and fancy dress optional

Distance: 360 ft (110 m)

Obstacles: Peat bog; trying not to laugh, as this may result in swallowing bog water

Cited by *Lonely Planet* as one of the top 50 things to do around the world in 2014, the bogsnorkelling championships, held at the Waen Rhydd bog around a mile from the town of Llanwrtyd Wells in mid-Wales, draw hundreds of competitors from all over Europe and as far afield as South Africa, New Zealand and Mali. Participants must snorkel to the end of a water-filled trench cut through the peat bog, using only leg power (no hands), and back again in the fastest possible time.

The event begins at 10 a.m. and, depending on the placement you are allotted, you may have to wait for 100 or so snorkellers to go before you, wondering if you have a chance of beating their time. Spectators (as well as competitors) can avail themselves of a real ale and cider bar throughout the day, as well as enjoying stalls and live music. Online entries close seven days before the event. Bob Greenough, one of the organisers, said, 'Part of the fun is making a fool of yourself.' The same trenches are used every year and are apparently home to fish and insects including water scorpions – which sound off-putting but aren't in fact dangerous at all.

The town came up with the event when a group of local businesspeople put their heads together in the 1970s to think up ways to draw people to Llanwrtyd Wells after the decline of pony-trekking tourism. Gordon Green, owner of the Neuadd Arms Hotel, was one of the leading figures. They staged the first ever Man versus Horse Marathon in 1980 (it took 25 years before a runner beat a rider on horseback). They now have over a dozen unusual 'Green Events', having expanded the bog-snorkelling events to include Mountain-Bike Bogsnorkelling and a Bogsnorkelling Triathlon.

In 2012 they held the first World Alternative Games, with over 2,000 people competing in such non-mainstream events as worm charming, husband dragging, stiletto racing, hay bale tossing, egg throwing, finger jousting and the World Bathtubbing Championships: *Lonely Planet* called it 'the coolest place to be' in 2014, when 60 events were staged over two weeks. Everyone taking part received a Corinthian medal.

You can also compete in bog-snorkelling events in Australia, Sweden and Ireland.

PROFILE

Just why are girls so good at snorkelling through dirty, cold and slightly smelly bogs? It remains a mystery, but the facts speak for themselves.

In 2013 Dineka Maguire won her fourth World Championship title in a row, at the age of 18, and she had also won the Junior World Championships in 2011 and 2012.

In 2014, 16-year-old Emma Pitchforth claimed the title of Junior World Champion and second place overall. Perhaps this is partly explained by the fact that her parents are both former bogsnorkelling winners. The whole family competed in 2014 – mum, dad and two brothers – and Emma also won gold in the underwater hockey team at the World Alternative Games. Her mother Joanne said, 'It was a novelty for Emma to beat her twin brother at something.'

Perhaps one explanation could be, in the words of a devotee of the sport who took part in the first bog-snorkelling championships in County Tyrone, Northern Ireland, in 2005: 'It's cold, yes, when you get in, but it's good for your skin.'

STATISTICS

 World Champion in 2014: Kirsty Johnson of Surrey (1 minute 22.56 seconds)

 Fastest man in 2014: Haydyn Pitchforth (1 minute 33.14 seconds)

 World Champion in 2013: Dineka Maguire (1 minute 23.13 seconds)

 Fastest man in 2013: David Williams (1 minute 32.68 seconds)

 Age of oldest competitor in 2013: 75 (bogsnorkelling without a wetsuit)

 Junior World Champion in 2014: Emma Pitchforth (1 minute 26.81 seconds)

 2014 prize for fancy dress: Suzanne Saunders, 'nurse shark'

FROZEN DEAD GUY COFFIN RACE

What is it? Team foot race with a coffin

Location: Colorado, USA

Established: Festival held since 2000

Held: Annually in March

Equipment: Box in the shape of a coffin (constructed of any materials)

Distance: Not known

Obstacles: One team member must be in the coffin

Six pallbearers carry a coffin with a rider inside, and the rider must be weighed to ensure they conform to minimum weight; all team members must wear a helmet. The object is to slide, roll, drag or carry a coffin through an icy obstacle course including climbs, mud and snow, without dropping it. The teams with the four fastest times race in the quarter finals, with the top two from that then racing for first and second place. It is recommended that the coffin have no top. The competition is limited to 30 teams and prizes are awarded for costumes, coffin design and team spirit. The race is part of a festival called Frozen Dead Guy Days, and there's quite a story behind it – something of a challenge in itself.

It starts in the year 1989 with the death, at the age of 89, of Bredo Morstoel, who had lived most of his life relatively anonymously in his native Norway, director of parks and recreation in the country's Baerum County for more than 30 years. Upon his death, his family took the rather unusual decision to preserve the body in dry ice and ship him to a California cryonics facility, in the hope that maybe one day technology would allow him to be brought back to life. Bredo's body rested there in liquid nitrogen for four years, until his daughter Aud and grandson Trygve moved him to the old mining town of Nederland, Colorado, with the idea of setting up in the cryonics business themselves, starting with Grandpa Bredo.

Then things started to get tricky. A municipal code against the keeping of frozen bodies on private property, such as the shed in the garden, threatened the family's plans. Aud was evicted because her home, lacking plumbing and electricity, violated local ordinances, and she would have to leave. Trygve had by this time met with visa difficulties and returned to Norway himself on a deportation order. Would the frozen dead guy be able to remain?

Well, thankfully the authorities of the mountain community that the *New York Times* called 'hippy-tinged' made an amendment to the law, and Grandpa Bredo was not only allowed to stay, packed in dry ice, in a shed, but became a media sensation. The town decided to celebrate their most famous frozen resident every year, giving Bredo a new life he would never have imagined. And thanks to the strange shenanigans of one Norwegian family in Colorado, you too can take part in the Frozen Dead Guy Coffin Race.

PROFILE

Dressed in pink shirts, short denim shorts and stripy pink knee socks, the Pink Socks team is made up of engineering graduates from the University of Colorado – six male pallbearers and one female 'corpse' – and team captain Joel Weber said back in 2012 when they completed the snowy and muddy course in just 50 seconds: 'Our jobs are just a way to fund our passion for coffin-racing.' Their coffin, however, is made from items found in a dumpster; Katie the corpse learnt early on that the worst part was the screws sticking into her as she was rolled around in the coffin. By the time they romped to a fifth victory in 2014, Joel said wryly of his now well-known team: 'We have our fans and we have our enemies, and we want to keep it that way.'

Manitou Springs in Colorado has the Emma Crawford coffin races in October. Emma Crawford had moved to Manitou Springs in the late 1800s, hoping to be cured of tuberculosis by the mountain air and fresh spring water. In spite of her illness, she managed to hike to the top of Red Mountain, an area she loved, and her wish was to be buried there if she succumbed to the illness, which she did. The townspeople carried her coffin up there.

Denton, Texas, introduced coffin racing to its own Day of the Dead festival in October, but this is a different style: racers drive their custom-made coffins like cars.

There is also a Frozen Dead Guy 50k (28.6 miles) that takes place in January in Nederland, held by the Human Potential Running Series. Run on icy dirt roads and trails from the Carousel of Happiness in Nederland to Chautauqua Park in Boulder, entrance to this event is free.

STATISTICS

 Minimum weight for team member riding inside the coffin: 75 lb (34 kg)

 Other events at the Frozen Dead Guy Days festival: Polar plunge, frozen salmon toss, ice turkey bowling

 Elevation of the town of Nederland: 8,230 ft (25,000 m)

 Population: Around 1,500

 Approximate number of festival-goers: 15,000+

? **GLEN NEVIS RIVER RACE**

What is it? A white-water rapids race on a lilo

Location: Fort William, Scotland

Established: 1973

Held: Annually in July

Equipment: Helmet, wetsuit, lifejacket and an inflatable 'craft' without sides

Distance: 2 miles (3.2 km)

Obstacles: Gurgling Gorge, Dead Dog Pool, the Leg Breaker and the Lower Falls Leap

The Lochaber Mountain Rescue Team based in Fort William, Scotland, is the busiest mountain rescue team in the UK with over 90 callouts per year. A team of around 40 hearty volunteers is on call all year round to rescue stranded walkers and climbers from Ben Nevis, the UK's tallest mountain, and the surrounding area. In 1973 they hit upon a plan to raise additional funds to support their vital and lifesaving work. They invited adventure seekers to attempt to navigate a 2-mile (3.2-km) stretch of freezing cold Glen Nevis rapids, on nothing but a lilo or other similar inflatable craft.

Every year the brave and, some might say, foolhardy, don crash helmets and wetsuits and hurl themselves off a narrow ledge into the river. The serious competitors typically take a traditional lilo, with the addition of some robust tape, to provide some extra handholds. Others opt for novelty inflatable craft including crocodiles, killer whales and the occasional sheep. The race includes a terrifying 30-ft (9-m) leap into a waterfall and a series of exhilarating swirling stretches of water before calming down in the gentler waters lower down in the Glen.

Timings vary dramatically every year depending on the speed of the water. In 2013, all 47 participants completed the course.

PROFILE

The Glen Nevis River Race attracts teams from a number of local businesses in the area and in 2011 the Underwater Centre in Fort William decided to enter a team. Their day job is all about providing training for divers working in the oil industry. Speaking to news reporters at the event, general manager Steve Ham said, 'We spend our working lives teaching people to be under the water. Today we're going to try to stay above it.' Steve might have been hoping to reap some benefits in staff morale as a result of taking part. 'I think these things are great to improve communications in the workplace.'

Student adviser Ingrid Vickers was another member of the Underwater Centre team in 2010, finishing in 53rd place. Smiling at the end of the race she listed her minor injuries to the waiting media but said the only real damage seemed to have been inflicted on her elegant manicure. 'A couple of fingernails have gone,' she said, 'and there's some bruises on the knees and probably on the hips as well, but I'll survive.'

STATISTICS

 Minimum fundraising target per competitor: £100

 Numbers of participants over the event's history:
Over 3,000

 Cash raised in 2003: £10,000

Results in 2013

 Fastest man: Craig McMahon, 36 minutes 43
seconds

 Fastest woman: Kyrie Barker, 49 minutes 41
seconds

? PENN STATE DANCE MARATHON

What is it? A 46-hour, no sitting, no sleeping, student dance marathon that raises millions of dollars to fight childhood cancers

Location: Pennsylvania, USA

Established: 1973

Held: Annually in February

Equipment: 8–10 pairs of socks, at least two pairs of sneakers, slippers, baby wipes, headband (optional)

Distance: No physical distance travelled but a huge emotional journey!

Obstacles: Fatigue, cramp and thousands of relentlessly cheerful Penn State students cheering you on

The 1969 film *They Shoot Horses, Don't They?* captured the bizarre craze that swept America during the 1920s and 1930s for dance marathons. In the depths of the Great Depression, hard-up couples competed for fame and prize money by seeing who could stay on their feet for the longest. Today in the USA, students continue to keep the tradition alive, raising heroic amounts of money for charity as they do.

The biggest fundraiser of them all is the Penn State Dance Marathon, known affectionately as THON. In the vast Bryce

Jordan Center, just over 700 dancers, many representing student societies, fraternities and sororities, strut their stuff for an entire weekend, without sitting down or sleeping at any point. While DJs, bands and celebrities donate their time to make the event, at its heart are the dancers themselves. On hand to support them is an army of volunteers, serving up food, drink, massages and motivational letters from the families of children affected by cancer.

While dancing styles must have varied dramatically from the first dance marathon in 1973, in which 39 couples participated, the main criterion is simply staying on your feet all weekend. The concept of the dance marathon has now spread to many other locations.

PROFILE

Cynthia Erickson participated in the Penn State Dance Marathon in 1981 with her friend Tim Sommer. Too junior to represent their respective sorority and fraternity houses, they entered as 'independent dancers'. Competition for places was less tough then and they just had to raise a $20 entry fee. Nowadays potential dancers have to commit to huge fundraising targets and win a coveted place in a university-wide ballot. Cynthia and Tim found a photographer who agreed to sponsor them in exchange for having his name on their T-shirts, and they were in. In her blog post on the THON Alumni web pages, Cynthia recalls that the dance was: 'HARD. We were required to keep moving during the whole thing and I had a hard time in the days afterward standing still without unconsciously swaying to some unheard beat.'

Competitors were allowed one three-minute bathroom break every eight hours. Four girls and four boys would run down the hall for the chance to sit down on the toilet and rest their legs. There was a slight sense of panic every time they heard that one of the exhausted dancers had dropped out or been carried off, and Cynthia and Tim wondered if they would be next. Cynthia wore earplugs to muffle the music and changed her shoes every four hours. In the final few minutes the DJ played 'Celebration' by Kool and the Gang and even the most exhausted among the dancers managed to kick it into gear for the finale.

Cynthia still keeps in touch with her dance partner Tim, who sends her a copy of the university newspaper every year on the Monday after the THON weekend.

STATISTICS

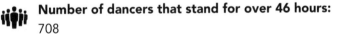 **Money raised by THON in 2014:** $13.3 million

 Number of dancers that stand for over 46 hours: 708

Penn State students who volunteer for THON annually: 15,000

THE WORLD'S TOUGHEST RACES

 Total combined length of all the sandwiches consumed during THON Weekend 2014: 1,200 ft (365 m)

 Number of meals served during THON Weekend 2014: 17,500

Water bottles handed out during THON Weekend: 28,234

 Number of committee members: 3,400

? WIFE-CARRYING WORLD CHAMPIONSHIPS

What is it? A foot race in which a man carries his wife

Location: Sonkajärvi, Finland

Established: 1992

Held: Annually in July

Equipment: Clothes that will not fall off under duress and which can be easily grabbed hold of; the man is allowed to wear a carrier's belt, the woman a helmet; bunch of birch switches, swimming goggles and swimming slippers

Distance: 832 ft (253.5 m)

Obstacles: Two log hurdles and a water obstacle 3 ft (1 m) deep

On the face of it, the outwardly jolly sport of wife carrying seems a world away from the blood, sweat and tears of your average endurance event. Yet despite the aura of humour that surrounds it – and even allowing for the fact that one of the rules of the sport is that competitors must enjoy themselves – competing couples take wife carrying deadly seriously.

Wife carrying originates in Finland, where it is known as *eukonkanto*. As with most great sports, its origins are at once distinguished and murky, although it is generally agreed that a late nineteenth-century outlaw by the name of Herkko

Rosvo-Ronkainen was integral to its genesis. According to folklore, Herkko led a band of thieves who terrorised villages and were particularly fond of including local women among their spoils. Needless to say, the majority of these women did not take kindly to being abducted and resisted stoutly. This, together with the fact that Herkko's men appear not to have possessed horses, meant that it was necessary for the outlaws to lug their captives away on their backs.

Colourful as it is, the legend of Herkko and his men plays on a national stereotype. History suggests that over the centuries Finns were inveterate wife stealers.

Nowadays wives volunteer for the pleasure of being carried. And while in the interests of teamwork it is recommended that a man carries his own wife, it is by no means mandatory. The only stipulations are that the woman to be carried is over 17 years of age and weighs at least 108 lb (49 kg). Underweight wives can be brought up to scale by being saddled with a suitably laden backpack, although given that first prize in the race is the wife's weight in beer, it stands to reason that the heavier the wife a man can manage, the better.

As to how a man carries his wife, that's up to the individuals concerned. Fashionable nowadays is the so-called Estonian method, in which the woman wraps her legs around the man's neck and hangs upside-down behind him. Effective as it is, the posture is tough on the wife who not only finds herself face first against her carrier's posterior, but also risks drowning in the water obstacle.

PROFILE

Among other details, the official website thoughtfully includes a section full of advice on 'how to become a master in wife carrying'.

Clearly the sport isn't as straightforward as it initially appears. While elements such as attitude (part humour, part tough competition) and rhythm (mutual is best) are easily grasped, other aspects of wife carrying cut right to the heart of human existence. According to the chap who composed this wisdom, wife carrying is nothing less than 'an attitude towards life'. People who engage in the sport, he suggests, remain undaunted by the sorts of challenges that bedevil lesser mortals. On the contrary, 'they push their way persistently forwards, holding tightly, generally with a twinkle in the eyes'. People who engage in the sport are remarkable for their 'placidity and happiness'.

Wife carrying, our man maintains, is also erotic. Though it may not look like it to the outsider, lying at the heart of the sport is the age-old relationship between man and woman. Carrier and carried must understand each other intuitively. It is also desirable that, throughout the course of the race, they merge as one. Additionally, and in case you were wondering what the bunch of birch switches listed in the equipment section was for, it appears that in the heat of battle a spot of whipping often proves salutary.

Given all that, it is preferable if the wife is your own, especially if she is 'harmonious' and 'gentle' and blessed with a good sense of balance. Teaming with your own wife may also assist in training, which, the author declares, can easily be slotted into the daily routine. Bathtubs, supermarkets, playgrounds and 'body-building centres' are all recommended as suitable training grounds.

STATISTICS

 Though a Finnish speciality, wife carrying is now well-established in the wider world. Every year qualifying events, in which both physical condition and sense of humour come under the microscope, are held in countries as disparate and far-flung as Britain, Hong Kong, Germany, Ireland, Australia, Estonia and the USA

 Estonians tend to dominate the sport, much to the displeasure of the Finns who consider it their own. The world record of 55.5 seconds is held by Margo Uusorg and Birgit Ulricht, who hail from the Estonian capital of Tallinn. Among Finns the record is 56.7 seconds, held by Jouni and Tiina Jussila from the town of Raissio in Southwest Finland

 In the 2014 event, British couple Rich Blake and Anna Marguerite Smith, winners of the UK's seventh annual Wife-Carrying Race, crossed the line a mere one second behind winners Ville Parviainen and Janette Oksman from Finland. The winning time was a leisurely 63.75 seconds

No mention of wife carrying would be complete without the names of Taisto Miettinen and Kristiina Haapanen who won the World Championship in a record five consecutive years, from 2009–13

? WORLD CHAMPIONSHIP PACK BURRO RACE

What is it? Race with a donkey

Location: Fairplay, Colorado

Established: 1949

Held: Annually on last weekend of July

Equipment: One burro laden with 33 lb (15 kg) of mining equipment

Distance: 29 miles (47 km)

Obstacles: Rugged terrain, climb of 3,000 ft (914 m) from the town of Fairplay to the 13,185 ft (4,018 m) summit of Mosquito Pass

Prominent on the website of the evocatively named Western Pack Burro Ass-ociation are the words *Celebrating 64 Years of Hauling Ass*. This explains in a nutshell the gist of the organisation's longest and arguably toughest event, the World Championship Pack Burro Race, the highlight of Fairplay's Burro Days summer festival and the quintessential celebration of the Wild West and the region's pioneering spirit.

For the uninitiated, *burro* is the Spanish word for donkey. And the World Championship Pack Burro Race is exactly what it says; a gruelling no-holds-barred contest in which competitors may lead, drag, push or carry, but under no circumstances ride, their favourite donkey over a demanding 29-mile (47-km) course. Further adding to the fun, the animal in question must be equipped with saddlebags holding 33 lb (15 kg) worth of equipment including a pick, a pan and a shovel.

Declared by local legislature 'a summer heritage sport in Colorado' in June 2012, burro racing has its origins in the gold-rush days of the 1800s. Back in those barnstorming days, prospectors carried their gear on the backs of burros when searching for gold, silver and other precious ores. At times, they would have to race back to town and the local assayer's office in order to stake their claims before anyone else (and then race back to the site).

According to one legend, the modern race began in 1949 in a Leadville saloon. Suitably charged on whisky and beer, a handful of miners had a wager on who could get themselves and their donkey fastest to neighbouring Fairplay. There is, however, another legend, far less romantic and more self-serving, that the race was the brainchild of local merchants seeking to draw more tourists to what was then Fairplay's 'Gold Days' celebration.

In any event, the winner of the inaugural Rocky Mountain Pack Burro Championship Race, Melville Sutton with his donkey Whitey, pocketed $500 cash and a trophy donated by the *Rocky Mountain News*. To all other finishers the bartender at Fairplay's Hand Hotel awarded a free carton of beer.

For many, getting your donkey to actually move constitutes the biggest challenge. The phrase 'stubborn as a mule' was not made in jest. Having achieved this, competitors next have to deal with the course: the length of an ultramarathon, it boasts more than 3,000 ft (914 m) of vertical gain and descent, a

2-mile ordeal across a high-altitude tundra field known as American Flats, two crossings of Mosquito Creek and a stiff climb through a rock glacier to the summit of Mosquito Pass.

PROFILE

The ongoing challenge to 'Get Their Ass Up the Pass' has, over the years, produced some phenomenal performances. By all accounts the 1960s provided some of the most stunning contests when nine-time winner Joe Glavineck and his fellow mining competitors found themselves pitted against professional marathon runners who, presumably, found the race a good opportunity to add another string to their bows. After winning his first race in 1955, Glavineck's special rapport with his burros kept him at or near the top for the next 20 years. He was a picaresque performer known for antics like getting down on his hands and knees and kissing the finish line.

The last true miner to win the race, in his time Glavineck took on and beat many of the best runners of his era including a number of Olympic prospects. His clashes with champion marathoner Steve Matthews were particularly noteworthy. Glavineck's ongoing success against Matthews provided ample proof, if any were needed, that running talent alone was not enough to win the race. A man also had to be able to handle his donkeys.

STATISTICS

 Number of competitors in first race: 19

 Number of finishers in first race: 13

 Winner of first race: Melville Sutton, 5 hours 10 minutes 41.2 seconds

 Record holder: Tom Sobal, 3 hours 44 minutes

 Average time to complete the course: Approx. 5 hours

 Record for the most race wins: Tom Sobal, ten wins (Sobal claimed the record with his victory in 2002, surpassing the nine wins of the legendary Glavineck)

 Prize money: $1,000

 Spectators in 2012, despite wet weather: 10,000

? EMPIRE STATE BUILDING RUN-UP

What is it? Running up the steps of the Empire State Building as fast as possible

Location: Manhattan, USA

Established: 1977

Held: Annually in February

Equipment: Running gear

Distance: 86 flights of stairs (1,576 steps)

Obstacles: The elevation: 1,454 ft, vertically

This one's sometimes called a vertical marathon, yet it's over in the time it takes to buy a coffee. It's tempting to think that New York's Empire State Building Run-Up's origins hail from a day when the elevator wasn't working. The elevator reaches the observatory tower in under a minute.

The 2014 event, which included 650 climbers, was hosted by the New York Road Runners, who run the New York Marathon. It is one of the best-known tower climbs in the world and attracts international runners. To prevent there being a crush of people in the stairwell, there's a series of start times beginning with the elite women's and men's groups.

Runner Tricia Williams said in 2014, her second race, 'By

the time you hit the sixtieth floor your heart's beating out of control,' but that the adrenaline keeps you going to the top.

For the six years up to 2015, the women's heat has been won by Suzy Walsham, an Australian who lives in Singapore, who was 41 when she won for the sixth time. Her 2014 time was faster, averaging 0.45 seconds per step.

PROFILE

Firefighter Touché Howard of Durham, North Carolina, completed the Empire State Building Run-Up in 2014. He had set it as a goal for himself after incurring a back injury on the job in 2008 at the age of 50, while carrying a woman suffering from a seizure. 'I didn't know if I would ever be a firefighter again,' he said.

His colleagues in the 12-strong squad supported him and worked hard to help him get back into shape, never letting him give up hope that he would one day be back on duty.

In contrast to those in skimpy gear who look as if they're at a particularly gruelling step class, Howard ran in around 60 lb (27 kg) of firefighting gear. Luckily this included his compressed air breathing apparatus. 'So that's in my favour... I will use every bit of it to get up there.'

His other goal was to raise $30,000 for the Multiple Myeloma Research Foundation. His battalion chief had been diagnosed with the bone marrow cancer and he admired what the organisation had achieved, and the way they inspired optimism. 'That's the sort of thing that firefighters thrive on, people pulling together and supporting each other,' he said.

He trained three hours a day for six weeks, using multi-storey car parks and 15-storey buildings in Durham. Completing the race dispelled his fear that he would never get back in firefighting shape again. He said the actual race was the worst uphill battle he had faced, but the view over the city and the cool air at the top made finishing a moving moment.

STATISTICS

 Fastest woman (2015): Suzy Walsham (Australia), 12 minutes 30 seconds

 Fastest man (2015): Christian Riedel (Germany), 10 minutes 16 seconds

 Fastest woman (2014): Suzy Walsham, 11 minutes 57 seconds

 Fastest man (2014): Thorbjørn Ludvigsen (Norway), 10 minutes 6 seconds

Records:

 Men's: Paul Crake (Australia), 9 minutes 33 seconds (2003)

WEIRDEST

 Women's: Andrea Mayr (Austria), 11 minutes 23 seconds (2006)

 Touché Howard's time, in firefighting gear: 34 minutes 45 seconds

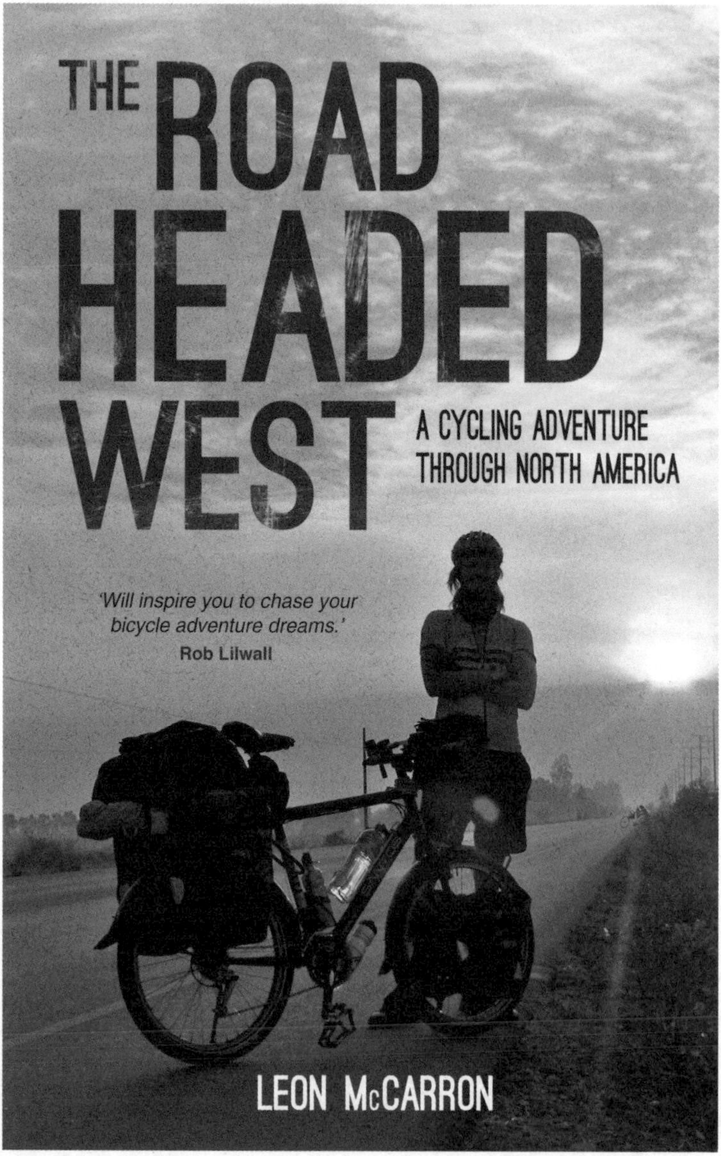
THE ROAD HEADED WEST
A CYCLING ADVENTURE THROUGH NORTH AMERICA
'Will inspire you to chase your bicycle adventure dreams.'
Rob Lilwall
LEON McCARRON

THE ROAD HEADED WEST

A Cycling Adventure Through North America

Leon McCarron

£9.99

Paperback

ISBN: 978-1-84953-635-6

'It seemed a terrible shame to meet my end in Iowa; I couldn't imagine anywhere more disappointing to die. If I were a betting man I'd have reckoned on the most dangerous thing in this state being sheer boredom. The scenery hadn't changed for weeks and I was slowly dissolving into stimulation-deprived madness. My current predicament, then – attempting to escape through cornfields from a gun-toting alcohol-soaked rancher – was not something I expected.'

Just months after graduating from university, Leon received disastrous news: he had been offered a job. Terrified at the prospect of a life spent behind a desk, without challenge or adventure, he took off to cross America on an overloaded bicycle packed with everything but common sense. Over five months and 6,000 miles, Leon cycled from New York to Seattle and then on to the Mexican border, facing tornados, swollen river crossings and one hungry black bear along the way. But he also met kind strangers who offered their food, wisdom, hospitality and even the occasional local history lesson, and learned what happens when you take a chance and follow the scent of adventure.

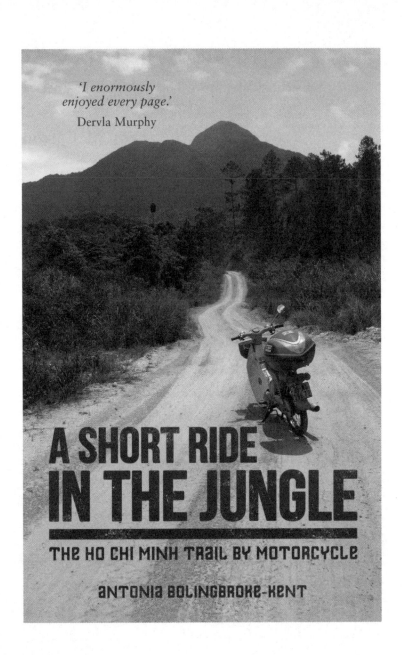

A SHORT RIDE
IN THE JUNGLE

THE HO CHI MINH TRAIL BY MOTORCYCLE

ANTONIA BOLINGBROKE-KENT

A SHORT RIDE IN THE JUNGLE

The Ho Chi Minh Trail by Motorcycle

Antonia Bolingbroke-Kent

£9.99

Paperback

ISBN: 978-1-84953-543-4

'For the first time in my life I felt that death was a possibility; a stupid, pointless, lonely death on the aptly named Mondulkiri Death Highway.'

The Ho Chi Minh Trail is one of the greatest feats of military engineering in history. But since the end of the Vietnam War much of this vast transport network has been reclaimed by jungle, while remaining sections are littered with a deadly legacy of unexploded bombs. For Antonia, a veteran of ridiculous adventures in unfeasible vehicles, the chance to explore the Trail before it's lost forever was a personal challenge she couldn't ignore – yet it would sometimes be a terrifying journey.

Setting out from Hanoi on an ageing Honda Cub, she spent the next two months riding 2000 miles through the mountains and jungles of Vietnam, Laos and Cambodia. Battling inhospitable terrain and multiple breakdowns, her experiences ranged from the touching to the hilarious, meeting former American fighter pilots, tribal chiefs, illegal loggers and bomb disposal experts.

The story of her brave journey is thrilling and poignant: a unique insight into a little known face of Southeast Asia.

'Practical, encouraging and funny –
the ideal guide for women looking
to get into triathlon'
Kate Carter, *The Guardian*

TRICURIOUS

Surviving the Deep End, Getting into Gear and Racing to Triathlon Success

**Laura Fountain
and Katie King**

TRICURIOUS
Surviving the Deep End, Getting into Gear and Racing to Triathlon Success

Laura Fountain and Katie King

£8.99

Paperback

ISBN: 978-1-84953-714-8

Laura was a self-certified couch potato who, until a few years ago, could only run for a couple of minutes at a time, and couldn't swim. She has now completed several marathons and is a committed triathlete.

But Laura couldn't have achieved what she has without the advice and support of her friend Katie. A life-long runner, fair-weather cyclist and born-again swimmer, Katie helped Laura through the ups and downs of training for a triathlon. As well as surmounting fears of failure and, more importantly, Laura's fears of drowning in the swim start, their triathlon journey gave them the opportunity to push their limits and have fun along the way.

Tricurious tells Laura's and Katie's story with energy and humour. Filled with anecdotes and advice about the trials and tribulations of preparing for a triathlon, this inspiring book will answer your questions and leave you curious to experience the joy (and pain) of swim, bike, run.

Have you enjoyed this book?
If so, why not write a review on your favourite website?

If you're interested in finding out more about our books, find
us on Facebook at **Summersdale Publishers** and follow us on
Twitter at **@Summersdale.**

Thanks very much for buying this Summersdale book.

www.summersdale.com